Jennifer Elison, Ed.D. (left), has been a grief and transition counselor in private practice since 1990. Chris McGonigle, Ph.D., is the author of *Surviving Your Spouse's Chronic Illness,* and her work has been widely published in national magazines. Both authors live in Montana.

Also by Chris McGonigle

Surviving Your Spouse's Chronic Illness

LIBERATING
～LOSSES

WHEN DEATH BRINGS RELIEF

JENNIFER ELISON, ED.D.
CHRIS McGONIGLE, PH.D.

Da Capo
LIFE
LONG
A Member of the
Perseus Books Group

Text design by Reginald Thompson
Set in 11-point Palatino by the Perseus Books Group

Cataloging-in-Publication data for this book is available from the Library of Congress.

First Da Capo Lifelong Books paperback edition 2004
ISBN13 978-0-7382-0948-7; ISBN-10 0-7382-0948-1

Published by Da Capo Lifelong Books
A Member of the Perseus Books Group
http://www.dacapopress.com

Da Capo Lifelong books are available at special discounts for bulk purchases in the U.S. by corporations, institutions, and other organizations. For more information, please contact the Special Markets Department at the Perseus Books Group, 11 Cambridge Center, Cambridge, MA 02142, or call (800) 255-1514 or (617) 252-5298, or e-mail special.markets@perseusbooks.com.

Table of Contents

Jennifer's dedication:
To my late husband, my shooting star.

Chris's dedication:
To Don.
Someday we'll sit "on the dock of the bay" together.

Jennifer's Acknowledgments

The idea of writing a book that examines the relief aspect of bereavement has been a professional and personal goal for many years. I am grateful to my collaborator, Chris McGonigle, for her belief in me and this project. Her gift of eloquent and compassionate writing has allowed us to expand the understanding of grief in a way that is both thought-provoking and comforting.

Our agent, Diana Finch, used her expert advice and knowledge to guide the development of the preliminary book proposal. She took a risk with a topic which is somewhat controversial, and skillfully sold the idea to a market replete with bereavement books.

Dr. Dan Tobin of the Life Institute is our true champion. From the first time he heard about the idea for a book about relief in the grieving process, he offered his support, even to the point of helping to sell this book idea to our publisher. Thank you, Dan.

Marnie Cochran, senior editor at Perseus, has been a godsend. Her wisdom and knowledge of human behavior, her impeccable writing skills, and her kindness have proven to be invaluable.

Dr. Pat Bomba, Excellus Medical Director, Geriatrics, of Rochester, New York, so embraced the idea of relief as a disenfranchised component of grief that she recruited interviewees for us via her quarterly newsletter.

The members of the Helena Life Transition Network represent not only professionals in the field of end-of-life care and bereavement but also community members who share an interest in those topics as well. Their belief in this project has been extraordinarily validating.

Ken Doka, Ph.D., Charles Corr, Ph.D., and Monica McGoldrick, Ph.D., all busy with academic duties and research obligations, shared their opinions, experiences, and advice and answered our many questions with grace and professional camaraderie.

Thank you, Ken Doka, for your diligent research, which resulted in the concept of disenfranchised grief. Without you, this book would not be possible.

We are grateful to all of the relieved grievers who honored us with the truths of their histories.

It is at times challenging to conduct research in a rural environment. We are grateful to the staff at the Lewis and Clark Library in Helena, Montana, and to Mary Ruof, reference librarian at the National Reference Center for Bioethics Literature, for their tireless assistance with obtaining articles and books and conducting reference searches.

To my husband and best friend, Brad, for his restful sense of equilibrium.

To my children, Emily and Gregory, who constantly remind me of my many blessings.

Chris's Acknowledgments

To our three angels, who saw the need for a book like this: Diana Finch, Marnie Cochran, and Dan Tobin. To my children, Megan McGonigle Gittings and Tim McGonigle, for understanding that "wealthy freelance writer" is the ultimate oxymoron, and for generally being two terrific kids; Jack and Elizabeth Caldwell, my parents, my two leprechauns, and my two biggest fans; Dottie Bowman, for our walking-and-talking therapy sessions, for which she never charged me a dime; my ever-patient and thoughtful sister-in-law, Mary McCourt; Tom Eastman, for knowing where to find anything, and always lending a capacious ear; Pat Trafton, for being a "wise woman" on a number of fronts; Charles Corr, Kenneth Doka, Monica McGoldrick; India Bauer, Jan Jahner, Karen Krissovich, and the other hospice nurses, who offered wisdom only those in the trenches acquire; Mary Kinzer-Johnson, Donna Wallace, Rev. Dan Shea, Patty White, Paulette Kohman, Denise Gleason, John Putch, Rabbi Earl Grollman, and the staff at the Lewis and Clark Library. To

ACKNOWLEDGMENTS

Jennifer, my coauthor, who has to be the easiest person to work with on the face of the earth. And certainly not least, heartfelt thanks to those who made this book possible by opening the intimate details of their lives to the scrutiny of two strangers.

Authors' note:
Some names have been changed to protect privacy.

Introduction

Jennifer's story:

In October 1999, I signed up for training in the Widow-to-Widow volunteer program, not suspecting it would change the course of my life.

The program, sponsored by AARP and a local hospital, trains widows and widowers to serve as resources and friends to those whose spouses have died recently. I was one of seven widows—no widowers this time—who signed up for it. One of the goals of the course is getting volunteers to feel comfortable telling their own stories, and so, early in the training, that is what we do.

There were three trainers, and Chris was one of them. I was struck by her explanation that "widow" comes from a Sanskrit word meaning "empty," or "poured out." Even sixteen years later, and happily remarried, I recalled hating the word "widow" and had never referred to myself as one. It never seemed to fit me; far from feeling empty, following the death of my husband, I felt full—full of life, full of hope, full of possibilities.

Notwithstanding my fear that I might be alone in my reaction to widowhood, I felt comfortable in this group. There were plenty of humorous moments, as well as the sense of comfort that flows from sharing experiences, and even though I couldn't relate to everything the others said, I certainly could identify with some of them.

When my turn came to talk, my mouth was dry and my heart pounded. "My first husband, Paul, and I did not have a good marriage . . ." I began. The quiet room got even quieter. I took a deep breath and plunged on, telling about the fairy tale–turned–horror story that had been my four-year marriage. I told about falling deeply in love with a man who seemed to epitomize everyone's idea of the up-and-coming young physician, and how I had thrown myself into becoming the perfect doctor's wife. Though universally admired by the community, my brilliant and handsome young husband had a dark streak he showed only to me. Finally unable to keep up the pretense anymore and continue to endure his criticism and neglect, I told him I was going to see a lawyer about a divorce. The day after that, Paul was dead, his small car crushed by a semi truck on a dark two-lane highway. A little shamefaced, I admitted to the group that what I felt, as I rode to the funeral in the back of the white limousine, was overwhelming relief.

Chris's story:

I liked Jennifer the moment I met her as a Widow-to-Widow trainee. She has one of those engaging personalities that instantly accepts people just as they are, and she sees humor in every situation. Her insights as a grief counselor, as well as her ready wit, were a welcome addition to the training. I was eager to hear her story. Surely her first husband must have treasured her—any man would have, I thought—and his death must have caused her great distress.

When her turn came to tell her story during the second day of the training, she seemed suddenly uncomfortable, and she hesitated before beginning. As she told of her disastrous marriage, and her positive emotions following her husband's death, I was a little shocked by her frankness—and a little worried about how the other widows might react. I realized that I had never heard a fellow widow admit to such a relationship. However, no one seemed scandalized, and I, for one, was impressed with Jennifer's honesty. *Good for you*, I thought, *for being true to yourself. Maybe this will allow the others to be equally honest about their own responses.* Many widows, me included, have a tendency to idealize their dead mates.

During the coffee break, Jennifer and I talked. I told her I admired her for being so brave; she confessed that this was the first time since her first husband's death that she had "come out" to a group. She had heard I was a writer and asked if I could advise her on a book she planned to write, which shattered the stereotype of the grieving widow. She talked about how alone she had felt after her husband's death, because none of the grief literature gave even a passing glance at "nontraditional loss response." "Everyone talks about 'the loved one,'" she told me plaintively. "But what if he was 'the unloved one'?"

I too had done a fair amount of reading on the subject of grief, and I knew what she meant by not fitting the mold. I had felt at times that my particular experience isolated me. My husband, Don, had died of a very long illness—fifteen grueling years' worth—and during that time, I did a great deal of "anticipatory grieving," as the experts call it. By the time he became a hospice patient, I had already buried, in my own mind, the vigorous, healthy husband I thought would be mine. Although hospice workers helped us enormously in many ways, I was sometimes uncomfortably aware that they found my lack of tears a little, well, unnatural. "It's okay to cry, you know," one of them reminded me gently, which only made me feel more conspicuous and guilty. When Don died a few years later, I felt a mix of emotions, with relief at the forefront. Yet I was astounded to read an "expert" who professed he did not believe in anticipatory grief. *Just what planet are you from, buddy?* I wondered. Obviously, he had never been in my shoes, and I wondered if he had ever had a grief experience at all.

After my conversation with Jennifer, I began to wonder about others who might have had similar experiences and recalled another time I had felt out of sync with expectations. I had gotten pregnant within a year of Don's diagnosis and was very upset about the pregnancy. *How*, I obsessed, *will we raise the two babies we have, with Don's health so uncertain?* When I miscarried at twelve weeks, I nearly wept with relief. Family and friends, particularly my own mother, were much more grief-stricken than I, which made me doubt my credentials as a good mother and a human being. And I wondered if they were right.

Who wouldn't want a beautiful new baby to cuddle? I wondered. *Am I a monster?* No, I decided, just a terrified young mother of a three- and a six-year-old who didn't want to bring another child into an already difficult situation.

Jennifer and I were atypical grievers in a society that assumes every death is a tragedy. Neither of us felt we would have been understood if we'd shared our true feelings, except, maybe, by those closest to us.

A big problem facing us while writing this book was that there is no name for all you relieved grievers out there. We didn't know what to call you! If you find yourself in this book, and you are discovering that many of your post-loss feelings are positive, you need to know that the language hasn't caught up with you yet. Considering that no one has studied you in any depth, this isn't surprising.

Let's look, for a moment, at the evolution of the word "bereaved," because it offers a perfect example of the way language has shaped our responses to death. "Bereaved" comes from Old English and means someone who has been "reaved," or "robbed," of something precious. Certainly, grief often feels that way: a terrible, unnecessary tearing from us of someone we loved. When we are bereaved, we feel beaten, bowed down, and beggared. The connotation of the word "bereft," a variant of "bereaved," implies someone who has been left with nothing at all. It is possible to feel like that after a death. But what if death has been not a robbery but a gift—both for the dead and for us? As linguists know, to name something is to have power over it. By naming an emotion, you do much more than simply apply a word to it. You identify it, own it, and gain mastery over it. Maybe someday English will make room for those who feel, not bereaved, but "begifted." When a word does not exist for an experience, the experience is discounted and dismissed. Being told your response doesn't exist implies that you don't either—not exactly reassuring!

In the aftermath of a death, you can feel as if you're going crazy. The English author C. S. Lewis once wrote that grief feels a lot like fear: the same sweaty palms, racing heart, repetitive thoughts, vivid nightmares. No wonder people look to prescriptions of all kinds, believing they are abnormal. If your reaction differs from what your friends, the grief books, the clergy, and everyone else thinks you should be experiencing, you have an additional burden to deal with—the expectations of others. The conflict that arises from feeling great relief alongside your sadness can be genuinely disorienting. And unfortunately, if your reactions don't jibe with those of your friends and relatives, you are not likely to get the comfort and support you need. Instead, you might hear things like, "I can't believe you're getting rid of his things already!" or, "She was such a great person. You must miss her terribly!" Obituary notices and clergy may describe your dead in ways you can't recognize. You may wince when you open condolence cards reassuring you that "the depth of your grief is equal to the depth of your love." Well-meaning people may tell you that you'll go through five stages of grief, even though they have little understanding of what that might mean. With so much misinformation, so many different loss situations, and so many different grievers, it's no wonder some people feel crazy!

Jennifer recently saw a woman in her grief counseling practice who asked her to do something to make her mad. "Why would you want me to do that?" Jennifer asked her, mystified. "My neighbor told me that at this stage, I should be angry, and I'm not," she confessed. "I'm afraid I'm not doing this right."

All of us are extremely aware of what others think, particularly after someone dies. We are a society with rigid, and often misguided, notions about what constitutes "correct" grieving. If there's one point we'd like to make in this book, it is this: Grief is a complex array of feelings and thoughts, encompassing every aspect of life—social, spiritual, intellectual, physical, and behavioral. After a death, we tend to question everything that has gone before, holding it up to the light of this new event. In some ways, our lives are poorer. However, a death can also mean that our lives change for the better, sometimes becoming a great deal better, and it's normal, natural, and desirable to acknowledge these good changes.

We wrote this book to reassure you that you aren't wrong because you're experiencing some good feelings now, feelings you may be having trouble acknowledging even to yourself. Maybe this is the only book you've picked up that even mentions relief in connection with death. Most don't. In these pages, you will meet people who had many different relationships with their dead, who were their mothers, fathers, children, in-laws, siblings, and spouses. The people who told us their stories experienced some of the aspects of traditional grief, such as sadness, pining, despair, and loneliness. But they also felt things they weren't "supposed" to feel: relief, peace, freedom, happiness, even joy. Sometimes they felt only these positive emotions; more often, they were mixed with darker feelings and thoughts.

Maybe you will recognize yourself in these pages. At least, we hope, you will realize that human experience leads us down many paths. Of all these experiences, grief is predominantly an emotional journey, and human emotions can never be predicted or corralled. Their glory, as well as their frustration, lies in the way they spring unbidden from deep within us.

They reflect the unique relationships we had with the dead, and if we listen, they tell us what it is to be fully, vibrantly human.

LIBERATING
LOSSES

1

Speaking Ill of the Dead

"They say you shouldn't say nothing about the dead unless it's good. He's dead. Good."

—Moms Mabley

Jennifer's story:

May is a beautiful month in Richmond, Virginia. The dogwood and azaleas vie to be the winner in Mother Nature's beauty contest. The air is ripe with the sweetness of new life and hope. The overwhelming beauty of spring creates a perfect backdrop for young love—and I was ready to fall in love. It was the spring of 1978 and I was twenty, working as a nurse's aide on a busy medical floor of a large urban hospital. Although my family now lived in New York, my mother had graduated from Virginia's Madison College, class of 1940, and had always wanted one of her children to follow in her footsteps. I was more than happy to fulfill her wish. I had spent summer vacations visiting my mother's relatives, and I had come to love the South. After enduring many blustery Northeast winters, I was drawn to the idea of daffodils blooming in February. I also looked forward to gracious Southern hospitality, a trait my mother had admired and tried hard to instill in her children. After my sophomore year at Madison, I transferred to the Medical College of Virginia to pursue a degree in nursing.

And though the professional experience I was gaining filled me with satisfaction and pride, there was something missing from my life. I was lonely for someone I could love, who would love me in return. When my cousin Jan, who worked in the same hospital as head nurse in the labor and delivery room, called to ask if she could arrange a blind date for me with a medical student, I was thrilled.

Paul was unlike anyone I had ever met. From our first date that spring, I was smitten. He was kind, compassionate, and intelligent. I admired his dedication to his studies and to his profession. He was a patient tutor, helping me understand the complexities of pharmacology and pathophysiology, two of the toughest subjects for any nursing student. His personality seemed to attract people to him, and he spoke with an authority people respected. It felt good and safe to be with him.

I fell head over heels in love and couldn't wait to tell my seven older sisters (we were a family of eight sisters and one brother) the happy news. So I had a difficult time understanding Paul's reservations about telling his parents about me. "Mother will ruin everything," was his response whenever I brought up the subject. A full year after we'd met, he introduced us at his commencement exercises from medical school. His mother's reception was cool. She seemed jealous of Paul's love for me, and as a Catholic girl from New York, from divorced parents, I did not fit her requirements as the prospective spouse of her only child. Naively, I told myself I could win her over, given time.

After graduating from nursing school, I decided to move to Norfolk, Virginia, and work at DePaul Hospital. My decision was based on the fact that Paul would be spending the next three years doing his internship and residency in the Tidewater area, and I wanted to be close to him.

I wish I could say our courtship was blissful, but it wouldn't be true. The ominous signs were there, but I was in a perpetual state of blind, heedless love. Medical school, internship, and residency are harshly demanding, and physicians keep long hours with little sleep. I excused Paul's irritability and emotional distance as the results of overwork. I became accustomed early on to a second fiddle role and tried not to be too demanding. After all, his professional dedication had been one of the qualities that drew me to him; it seemed hypocritical to complain about it now. How could I feel jealous when a sick patient intervened in our plans to be together? I made allowances for his mother, too; Paul was her only child. In my deluded state, I believed that once Paul's residency was over, all would be well.

We were married in May 1981 in picturesque Williamsburg, Virginia, in a historic colonial church. People told me it was the most magnificent wedding they had ever attended. I had dreamed of being married in my mother's lovely backyard garden, walking down a pathway of flowers, clutching a small bouquet of wild daisies, but those plans were quickly scuttled by Paul's family. Status and prestige were more important to them—and, it pained me to admit, to my future husband—than any of my wishes. It began to dawn on me that Paul, rather than disappoint his mother, would disappoint me. Our wedding was a production straight out of Hollywood, a display of pomp and circumstance designed to impress. Even more disheartening, Paul told me we should skip the honeymoon because he was afraid to leave our expensive wedding gifts in our condominium. He hadn't insured them yet, he fretted, and they could be stolen. When he saw my stunned face, he reluctantly gave in. I heaved a silent sigh of relief as we headed to the airport for St. Thomas.

Again, I swallowed my hurt, telling myself that there really would be a happily ever after once he finished his residency and we moved to a new town. Nothing could have been further from the truth. We moved to a tiny town in south-central Virginia on our one-year anniversary. Paul was the only physician within a sixty-mile radius of the hospital. When he wasn't making morning rounds or evening rounds, he was seeing patients in his office. When he wasn't seeing patients, he was out on a rescue-squad call. He was constantly exhausted, and his tendency to find fault with me intensified.

The loneliness and isolation that came with being a small-town doctor's wife was only a piece of my unhappiness. Paul and I fought daily about his expectations of me as a wife, and I watched my world shrink as he forbade me to go back to work or to school after the birth of our daughter. I could count on both hands the number of times we'd had sex in the four years we'd been married. The fact that I conceived during this time struck me as purely miraculous. Elizabeth was the one good thing to come out of my marriage. Paul often laughed at my attempts at seduction, and many nights I cried myself to sleep, wondering why he had married me at all.

No one knew of our crumbling Camelot. People saw us as the ideal young couple, and we strove to put the best face on things in public. But the effort left us weary and sick at heart. Paul's unhappiness grew into what I know now was a clinical depression, but he refused to seek treatment. What if someone found out we weren't the perfect little family we seemed, that he wasn't the perfect husband and father? Instead, he medicated himself with Valium and other prescription medications, and I grew more desperate than ever to keep him functioning and our family together.

I was only twenty-seven, but I felt my life was over. I couldn't face the thought of thirty or forty more years of marital hell. On January 21, 1985, I told Paul I wanted a divorce. The next day he was dead, killed almost instantly when his compact car hit a semi truck on a lonely stretch of Route 360. He was thirty-one.

For three nights following his death, I lay awake, agonizing over questions that buzzed in my brain like angry hornets. *Was I to blame for his accident? Had I so upset him that he wanted to end his life?* The thought of him choosing to kill himself was more than I could bear. That morning, he had kissed our toddler daughter as he strode out the door. "I'll see you when I get home tonight," he called.

Those didn't sound like the words of someone who planned on not returning. Still, the thought of suicide reverberated through my mind. We were both distraught over my decision to end the marriage, although this was not the first time we had discussed separating. Paul himself had threatened to leave me several months earlier, so it didn't seem to be a question of whether so much as when. This time, however, I had initiated the breakup, and I planned to move out. My heart clutched at the thought: *Was his death my fault?*

Or could he have had a heart attack? The previous summer, he had experienced an episode of intense chest pain. He had been doing heavy yard work, cutting down trees that had grown over the backyard pool. Suddenly, he fell to the ground, writhing and yelling for me to get the nitroglycerine tablets in his medical bag. Gradually, his pain eased, and with the immediate crisis over, he ignored my urging to get medical attention, despite his strong family history of heart disease. *So maybe*, I reasoned, *he died before his car hit the truck.*

I knew he had been exhausted. Neither of us had slept well the night before, and his typical workday was grueling. He drove the sixty-mile round-trip to the hospital twice a day to make rounds, in addition to seeing forty or fifty patients a day in his private practice. Late-night runs with the rescue squad added to his sleep deprivation. Earlier on that fatal evening we had met for dinner near the hospital, and I had noticed how haggard he looked as he confessed that he dreaded making evening rounds. He truly looked gray with fatigue, and I felt sorry for him.

The day after the accident, I asked one of his friends to come with me to retrace the route he had taken. *How could it have happened?* I asked myself, searching the bare highway for clues. But the glass and debris had been swept away, and not even a skid mark remained. I came home more baffled than ever.

After a few agonizing days of waiting, the medical examiner called, saying that, in his opinion, Paul had fallen asleep at the wheel. I was relieved to adopt his pronouncement. As much as I had wanted to end my marriage, I never wanted Paul to die. And I told myself that, whether the examiner was right or wrong, none of us would ever know the truth, so tormenting myself with guilt was futile.

In all the times I had thought about the future, I had never guessed that I would be granted a God-given divorce. We were both young and, for the most part, healthy, and I had no reason to believe Paul would die for many years. Yet it had happened, and I had to admit that the accident had solved our problems—his and mine— once and for all.

I could tell my mother and sisters about my true feelings because they knew, although I tried to spare them the worst details, how miserable my marriage had been. Because I was the youngest daughter, they were protective of me, so I had never talked too much about the depths of my misery. Now, outside of my immediate family, there was no one else I could talk to. "Never speak ill of the dead" is a strong cultural taboo; it's especially strong when the dead is one's young husband, and strongest of all when the husband was worshiped by the whole community.

Paul's compassion for his patients and their families had been the complete opposite of the way he treated me, and I was painfully aware that even if I had been brave or foolish enough to try to tell others about "my Paul," I wouldn't have been believed. How could the same person, my husband, turn such different faces to the world? I doubted my reality, and that in turn made me doubt my sanity.

From my nursing background, I knew that, because human beings are both private and public creatures, there are both private and public components to grieving. Most people grieve the way they live; extroverted personalities will grieve noisily and publicly, and introverts will grieve quietly and privately.

Unfortunately for me, if there were an "extroversion scale," I would be a 10. I am noisy with my feelings and exuberantly emotional; I wear my heart on my sleeve. So having to grieve one way in private and another in public was particularly difficult for me; in fact, it was exhausting. Much of my energy went into grieving "correctly." I was acutely aware that I was expected to adopt a Jackie Kennedy demeanor, but my alter ego was Scarlett O'Hara. With a pang of recognition I recalled the scene in which Scarlett, following the death of her first husband (whom she married, you recall, in a fit of pique when her beloved Ashley rejected her for Melanie), attends a ball in her widow's weeds. Southern society of the day forbade a new widow from dancing, but the camera zooms in on her foot, tapping away under voluminous black skirts as she eyes the dancers enviously. Like Scarlett, I was torn. In the eyes of the community, I took care to act like a properly grieving widow; inside, I was thankful that the marriage was over and that my and my daughter's futures would be healthier and, I was certain, happier.

Partly for solace, partly out of curiosity, I began a search of the grief literature, wondering what the "experts" had to say, or at least whether others had felt this way. *Surely*, I thought, *I am not the first one to find my own grief response at odds with the rest of the world. Surely these researchers and therapists have encountered a case like mine. Surely not everyone is saddened by a death.* But I was in for a shock. Both the popular and professional literature reinforced expectations that people grieve "a loss." Overwhelmingly, it was assumed that all bereaved people are mourning "a loved one" and suffering the same degree of emotional pain and turmoil. I discovered that some progress had been made. While anger had once been a forbidden emotion, in recent years author Elisabeth Kübler-Ross's work with the dying had made it acceptable to be angry at God, at life, at the deceased. She, more than anyone else, had taken death out of the closet and put it on the coffee table. However, her paradigm of the grief process—which she claimed encompassed the steps of denial, anger, bargaining, depression, and acceptance—had become prescriptive in our one-size-fits-all culture. But none of those fit me.

Looking back, I realize my situation was extreme. However, I believe that twenty-first-century America is a difficult place for anyone to grieve. All of us go unsupported, both in large ways and small.

According to the Bible, "The memory of the just is blessed: but the name of the wicked shall rot" (Proverbs 10:7). Yet we have to wonder if the Good Book got it wrong somehow. In this country, the dead undergo a transformation, starting with the obituary, continuing with the funeral ritual, and lasting into the indefinite future. No matter the person's real character, when he dies everyone works at forgetting his flaws and joins in a concerted effort to smooth out all the wrinkles.

In understanding modern death customs, it helps to think of the funeral as a drama in which all the participants play a role. In this way, funerals resemble other rituals, which are designed to comfort and reassure. One of our expectations as spectators is that the dead will go to heaven. Clergy have the job of ushering the deceased's soul into heaven, but more important, they must convince mourners of the person's entitlement to that realm, a task that sometimes requires no little finesse. Kathy Charmaz, professor of sociology at Sonoma State University, notes in *The Social Reality of Death* that the funeral eulogy is delivered to an audience "that probably knows potentially discrediting information that could cast doubt on their qualifications for 'everlasting life.' Hence, the clergy must construct the transformation between the persons known in the past to the *now sacred dead.*"

If clergy are the stars of the drama, funeral directors are the producers, going to great lengths to make sure everything proceeds as decorously as possible. Elaborate care is taken to give the illusion that the corpse is merely sleeping and that he or she will awaken soon in a better place.

Though other rituals are allowed some leeway, funerals are lockstep in the formulas they follow. British grief researcher Colin Murray Parkes has said that funerals are valuable in part because they assign new roles to the bereaved, "who may be suffering from the loss of their previous roles and functions." Wittily, Judith Martin (Miss Manners) calls the funeral "the most harshly appraised type of gathering held, and there is not, as after a botched dinner party, the possibility of erasing the failure by doing it over again, right." The "success" of a funeral derives in large part from how carefully everyone sticks to the script.

In this setting, even small deviations from the norm are noticed. No one's expectations must be thwarted, because that would cause additional distress in the face of an already deeply unsettling event. People tend to dress similarly, in subdued colors; a predictable format is followed, and only certain hymns are played or sung. Chris's mother remembers a funeral at which "Let Me Call You Sweetheart" was played as mourners left the church. It may have been the dead woman's favorite song, but the mourners commented on its oddness in that setting.

According to Kenneth Doka, senior consultant to the Hospice Foundation of America and professor of gerontology at the College of New Rochelle, death customs in America clearly favor family members. The closer the blood tie, the greater the loss is assumed to be, an assumption that, he believes, renders certain bereaved persons "disenfranchised." Doka coined the term in 1989 to describe a loss, or a person experiencing such a loss, that cannot be openly acknowledged, publicly mourned, or socially supported. "The history of it is simple and intriguing," he says. "I was teaching a class in the early to mid-eighties and we were talking about widows. And one woman said, 'If you think widows have it tough, you ought to see what happens when your ex-spouse dies.' I ended up doing research that started a chain of pieces of research that looked at what happens when grief is not recognized or acknowledged. The term 'disenfranchised,' and it really has a social, political origin, means that you really don't have a right to grieve."

Doka believes there are three types of disenfranchisement: (1) the relationship is not recognized (a former husband, for example, or a homosexual partner); (2) the loss is not recognized (an early miscarriage or an abortion); or (3) the grieving person is not recognized. The huge number of Americans cohabiting, or involved in homosexual partnerships, results in many disenfranchised grievers when one of the couple dies. Other unsupported grievers may be children, who are thought to be too young to understand the finality of death; the very old, who may have cognitive or memory deficits; and the developmentally disabled, who may be thought to lack the capability of grieving. And we are only beginning to realize that the loss of a pet can be severely traumatic, particularly for the elderly.

In an article for *OMEGA: Journal of Death and Dying*, Charles Corr, professor emeritus of philosophy at Southern Illinois University and author of several books on bereavement and death customs, has enlarged the concept of disenfranchisement. We often hear criticism, he says, of a range of grief behaviors, from the manner in which someone grieves ("She doesn't have to go to the cemetery every day. It's morbid.") to the length of time spent grieving ("Aren't you over this yet? It's been three months.") to the object being mourned ("It was only a cat, for heaven's sake!").

In the same way, certain grievers are seen as "enfranchised," or having a legitimate right to feel and act bereaved. No one disputes the rights of spouses, parents, siblings, grandparents, or others related by marriage, to take time off work, receive sympathy cards and flowers, and generally be treated deferentially because of their loss. The privileges of bereavement also bring responsibilities. Because bereaved people are so uncomfortably aware of social expectations, they may find themselves talked into buying the most expensive casket and the most elaborate funeral trappings. At no other time, it seems, is there more pressure to look and act in a certain way.

The pressure to conform goes beyond the immediate family to extended family, friends, and neighbors. Much of the reassurance we get from a funeral comes from the knowledge that, no matter how gruesome, sudden, or agonizing the death, the dead person is now beyond harm. In order to have made that journey, he or she must have had the right credentials. Taking our cues from clergy and funeral workers, we understand that direct criticism—no matter how objectionable the deceased's character—is forbidden. What is not said is often more revealing than what is. A woman we know recalls a funeral at which an elderly neighbor's several grown grandchildren were invited to get up and recall a fond memory of their grand-mother. An awkward pause followed when no one stepped forward. One minister asked if we had heard the old joke about one of his brethren who asked the funeral congregation if they had something good to say about the dead man. One man stepped forward and averred, "His brother was worse!"

If reminiscences are shared, the deceased's worst flaws are likely to be recast as charming foibles. Statements like, "We all know that Doris could be particular in her tastes," or, "George had a way of letting people know how he felt," tend to draw affectionate chuckles in this setting rather than the criticism they provoked in life. An acquaintance admitted to Chris that once, in the distant past, a man he sat next to at a funeral made no bones of what he thought of his deceased neighbor: "Seymour was a son of a bitch when he was alive, and he's a son of a bitch now." Statements like these are heard so rarely that the hearer is likely to remember them for a long time, as this man had.

Family and close friends are carefully scrutinized for evidence of "appropriate" grieving. In some cases of suspicious death, the husband or wife who grieves too little—or too much—has become the subject of a murder investigation. Whether John and Patsy Ramsey are ever found guilty in the death of their six-year-old daughter, JonBenét, their peculiar lack of affect following her murder has convicted them in the court of public opinion. Americans don't like people who don't "grieve right"—especially parents of young children. Likewise, a person who had no contact with the dying person but suddenly appears at the funeral wailing hysterically is likely to be the subject of derision. At the very least, deviations can set tongues wagging. Ironically, etiquette maven Judith Martin seems to have the most realistic picture of what grief looks like. "Both true grief and the absence of grief are, in their natural states, socially intolerable. Either joyous relief, or the ricocheting between hysteria and hilarity that is the natural reaction to deeply felt loss, is mistakenly perceived as an unnatural reaction."

Americans are uncomfortable with strong emotion, particularly sadness, and our funeral customs reflect our need to keep it in check. Maybe the popularity of confessional TV talk shows comes from being able to watch people emote at a safe distance. A funeral director we interviewed admitted he preferred ceremonies that emphasized the liturgy and discouraged personal references to the deceased. "I don't like it when things get out of control," he said, voicing the general sentiment. Jennifer remembers hearing a doctor in the hospital in which she worked order Valium for the family of a man who had died, because he felt their wailing was creating a disturbance. Certainly, it disturbed him.

We have adopted a kind of somber dignity as the ideal bereavement demeanor. After her husband's assassination, Jackie Kennedy became an icon of this kind of grief. The histrionic tearing of hair and rolling on the ground that is encouraged in other cultures is taboo here. However, tears are expected, and dry eyes may be remarked upon, even if the death has been long anticipated. In Chris's case, she felt she had cried all her tears during her husband's long illness, and she did not cry at his funeral.

She remembers a surreal moment just before the funeral, while she stood in the church vestibule chatting with the funeral director. He was chuckling over a minor fender-bender he'd had with one of the limousines on the way to the church. Chris joined in, but when the door opened and mourners entered, she worried that they might have observed her "unwidowlike" behavior. A giddy bride, she realized, would be forgiven; a giddy widow, never.

Obituaries sometimes go to ridiculous lengths to describe the deceased in terms so glowing, acquaintances have a hard time recognizing the person they knew. A mediocre marriage is transformed, by sleight of pen, to "she was the light of his life." Troubled parent-child relationships are rewritten as "he didn't spare the rod, but his children respected him." Hyperbole abounds. One woman was said to have taken in "homeless little animals and turned them into blue-ribbon champions." In another instance, a man who had been the next-door neighbor of an elderly woman—described as "always baking cookies for the neighborhood children"—recalled sourly, "Not for us, she didn't!" Eulogies can be just as mendacious. A woman who attended the funeral of her abusive, alcoholic brother, stunned by the flowery tributes, told us she felt "she had stumbled into the wrong funeral." And we recall an instance in which a local drug dealer, shot in the back by a disgruntled customer, was compared by his minister to Christ, because "he had followed his own path" and "was cut down in the prime of life."

Ironically, the attempt to make the individual more than he or she was has the opposite effect. What we love, and grieve, about each other is our uniqueness—precisely what is lost when obituary writers overreach themselves. Although the perfect world an obituary creates may fail to reassure, readers nevertheless take comfort in the facts it contains. *He fell out of a duck blind? Thank God, I don't have a duck blind! I don't even hunt! Cancer? I gave up cigarettes thirty years ago. She was eighty-seven? Whew, still twenty-three years to go!*

One might wonder, reading modern obituaries, if those described are really dead. The word is hardly used. Though our culture seems to have lost its ability to be shocked by four-letter words, "dead," "death," and "died" have come to sound increasingly obscene. The wonderfully onomatopoetic word "dead," bracketed by those two uncompromising *d*'s, comes from Old English, the language of the English peasant class, no strangers to the brutal unpredictability of life. In America today, top-heavy with an aging population, it would seem that the word would be embraced, as a generation of baby boomers glimpses the end of the trail. Alas, this honest Anglo-Saxon word is being replaced by all kinds of silly euphemisms. Most people these days "pass away," reminding one of a Noel Coward play, in which spirits in diaphanous dress come and go on cue. Some "pass," as if life were an extended exam. Some are "entered into rest," like an envelope through a mail slot, "go to their heavenly reward" (how does anyone know this?), or are "safe in the arms of Jesus," as if Jesus were an umpire in some cosmic baseball game. Jennifer's physician husband sometimes talked about a "negative patient outcome."

To be fair, these terms may not be just an attempt to pretty up an ugly fact; their slipperiness also reflects how slippery death has become. Formerly, it was said to have occurred when the heart stopped; now, it is pronounced only when there is no brain activity. Doctors are able to maintain someone on life support indefinitely to give kin time to say good-bye. In fact, we have many ways of postponing the end and great difficulty in knowing precisely when it occurs. Whatever the reasons for the abandonment of the "D-word," we feel strongly that using the actual terms is an important step in accepting the finality of death.

Trying to deny the harsh knowing that "dead" implies, we go to lengths to avoid it. Cultural historian Philippe Aries has noted that modern Americans are in search of the "tame death," that is, one that is private, calm, and sanitized. We shut the dying away in hospitals and hospices, then shun the bereaved until they behave normally again. Our attempts to suppress extravagant emotional displays, pretty up the language of death, and hurry along the grieving process are evidence of our current "death phobia." As Aries said of twentieth-century death customs, "one must avoid . . . the overly strong and unbearable emotion caused by the ugliness of dying and by the very presence of death in the midst of a happy life, for it is henceforth given that life is always happy and should always seem to be so."

Do it right but get it over with is the message society sends grievers—implying that there is an exact formula for "correct" grieving. If your grief seems like too much or too little for the others around you—and they are only too happy to let you know it—you begin to doubt your sanity. But don't look to family and friends to help. Those most in need of comfort can't always count on getting it—a trend that seems to be getting worse. Funeral customs make it harder for everyone—traditional and nontraditional grievers alike—to deal with loss. The tendency, when writing an obituary, to whitewash the quirks that made the deceased human; the increasing use of memorial services, or eliminating services entirely, which denies others the chance to mourn the death when their grief is fresh, or to see the body in the casket—a critical first step in grief recovery; the departure of friends and family immediately after the funeral—all these are ways we abandon the grieving. Widows, especially, complain that neighbors and friends "drop the casseroles and run," so that, when the painful reality begins to sink in, weeks or months later, they are alone.

It is fascinating to look at the way grief research has influenced our perceptions about "normal" grief. Large survey-type studies have focused almost exclusively on traditional manifestations of grief, maybe in part because researchers are fearful of angering subjects. The authors of one book confessed, "When we first considered asking the people in our bereavement study if they found anything positive in their loss, we were somewhat reluctant to do so. We were concerned that we would cause them further distress or offend them." Although some researchers give passing notice to "unresolved" or "complicated" grief, briefly acknowledging that some relationships are "ambivalent," no one has undertaken the study of relief death exclusively. Noted grief researcher Therese Rando, in her book *Treatment of Complicated Mourning*, asks subjects about their relationships, both the positive and negative aspects, with the dead, as well as how the survivor felt following the death. However, it is unusual to find a mention of "relief," even when the relationship can be assumed to have been troubled—say, in the case of suicide. In grief research, as in other fields, researchers have found what they expected to find, and because they have assumed that death is always a loss, they have found signs of traditional grief. The question "What don't you miss about this person?"—which Jennifer has learned to ask in her counseling practice—has been conspicuous in its absence. Studies list the overwhelming number of those who experienced "depression," "searching," "physical symptoms," and "crying spells," efficiently draining the emotional palette of color.

At long last, that approach may be changing. In a large study of married couples called Changing Lives of Older Couples (CLOC), conducted by the Institute for Social Research at the University of Michigan in Ann Arbor, researchers looked at the quality of the marital relationship prior to the death of one of the couple. They state unequivocally that "all losses are not equal; adjustment to widowhood is most difficult for those experiencing high levels of warmth . . . and low levels of conflict in their marriages." They conclude that "those who suffered conflicted marriages evidenced lower levels of yearning." However, they caution against assuming that a relationship was not loving simply because the griever does not seem to be exhibiting traditional grief behavior. They warn that such assumptions could be hazardous to the griever's mental health—certainly a warning that an aging society should heed.

Jennifer had her own moment of truth. In the spring of 1993, she was invited to be a guest speaker for a local group of Compassionate Friends, a support group for parents who have lost a child. Although she specialized in bereavement issues, she felt somewhat inadequate to speak to this group. Though every death is traumatic, there is something unthinkable about the death of a child, and because Jennifer had never lost a child, she felt somewhat out of her depth. However, because of her own non-traditional loss, her approach in her counseling practice had been to treat the grief experience holistically and explore all the components, including relief. And though relief wasn't something she would normally expect following a child's death, it was still possible. *A parent feeling relieved about a child's death would be full of conflict*, she thought, *and relief isn't something you can keep hidden from yourself.*

There was a great variety of child loss represented: stillbirths; children who had died as adults; children who had committed suicide; SIDS deaths. Every face looked hungry for comfort.

She began with an explanation of the traditional feelings of loss, then ventured into the nontraditional feelings. Instantly, she could feel the mood in the room change. Faces turned stony, and two women in the back exchanged glances. One man swore, sotto voce, "Well, mine wasn't!" when she suggested that some of these children were difficult. If they hadn't been constrained by politeness, she realized, they would have escorted her from the room, and quickly; in fact, if she'd been an out-of-town salesman, she would have been tarred and feathered and run out of town on a rail—that's how irate these parents were. Hastily summing up, she thanked them and left.

Much to her surprise, over the next few months she ran into some of the group in the grocery store, in the mall, and at the library, and their responses were very different. One thanked her for giving her permission to feel the relief she had been so ashamed of. Another told her, over a display of cantaloupes, that her son had been into drugs since he was twelve, and she no longer had to fear a phone call in the middle of the night. Jennifer was amazed and—she had to admit—gratified at having her hunch confirmed, and she was struck by the contrast between the parents as a group and as individuals.

The experience was a turning point for Jennifer, as she began to understand that many people, like her, are ashamed of some perfectly normal thoughts and feelings following a death.

2

Altruistic Relief

"To Arnold. Peace at last. From all his neighbors and friends."

—Newspaper obituary notice

It used to be that when someone died the only safe thing to say was, "I'm sorry." Etiquette books, talk-show hosts, even Dear Abby cautioned against these verbal gaffes: "You'll have other children." "God must have needed more angels in heaven." "It must be God's will." "I know just how you feel." "Just accept it and move on." Most of us, especially those who study the field, have been indoctrinated, many times, in what *not* to say. So when a colleague of ours heard of the death of an elderly neighbor, he knew that the only acceptable response was, "I'm sorry." He was surprised to hear the man's son demur. "Oh, don't be," he said. "Dad had suffered so long. It's really a relief."

More and more, three little words pop up following a death: "It's a relief." On the spectrum of positive emotions, "altruistic relief" is the most socially acceptable, because its basis is other-centered; the survivors are grateful the person is no longer suffering. Although the experience of grief has been with us as long as humankind, the study of it is a recent phenomenon. In this century, two researchers deserve special mention. On November 28, 1942, a nightclub called the Cocoanut Grove in Boston became a horrifying inferno when a busboy lit a match that caught the flammable furnishings on fire. Four hundred ninety-two people died, many of them servicemen and their dates celebrating the Thanksgiving holiday. The tragedy, occurring less than a year after the bombing of Pearl Harbor, made real the horrors occurring abroad in Europe and Asia. The work of Erich Lindemann, chief of psychiatry at Massachusetts General Hospital, who interviewed 101 survivors of the fire, helped millions understand their reactions to the wartime losses of their young husbands, brothers, and friends. Lindemann helped the grieving American populace understand that confusion, crying, digestive disturbances, and searching for the deceased are normal signs of grief.

Twenty-five years later, an Austrian-American physician, Elisabeth Kübler-Ross, performed a similar service for the children of Lindemann's generation by shedding light on the emotional fallout of another war: Vietnam. She wrote about the dying patients she observed in her work, and her book *On Death and Dying*, published in 1969, launched the hospice movement in America. Though her study was anecdotal rather than quantitative, and her subjects the dying rather than their survivors, her stage-based approach caught on immediately and has had enormous influence and durability. Kübler-Ross theorized that those facing death moved through five distinct stages: denial, anger, bargaining, depression, and acceptance. Maybe the ultimate testimony to the popularity of her five-stage model came when paterfamilias Homer Simpson of TV's *The Simpsons* cycled through them on a recent episode.

At the hospital, Homer, who has eaten a bad piece of sushi, sits on an examining table in his underwear, and Dr. Hibbert and Homer's wife, Marge, come in.

> Dr. H: *You have twenty-four hours to live.*
>
> Homer: *Twenty-four hours!*
>
> Dr. H: *Well, twenty-two. I'm sorry I kept you waiting so long. [Homer embraces Marge]*
>
> Dr. H: *Well, if there's one consolation, it's that you will feel no pain at all until sometime tomorrow evening, when your heart suddenly explodes. Now, a little death anxiety is normal. You can expect to go through five stages. The first is denial.*
>
> Homer: *No way! Because I'm not dying! [hugs Marge]*
>
> Dr. H: *The second is anger.*
>
> Homer: *Why you little . . . ! [steps toward Dr. H]*
>
> Dr. H: *After that comes fear.*

Homer: What's after fear? What's after fear? [cringes]

Dr. H: Bargaining.

Homer: Doc, you gotta get me out of this! I'll make it worth your while!

Dr. H: Finally, acceptance.

Homer: Well, we all gotta go sometime.

Dr. H: Mr. Simpson, your progress astounds me. [hands Homer a pamphlet, "So You're Going to Die."]

Black humor aside, Kübler-Ross's work paved the way for new theories about grief. Although her paradigm of five orderly stages has been widely criticized in recent years, she breathed new life into the subject of death and dying and introduced less sanctioned emotions, such as denial and anger, into the mix. In so doing, her work has made this book possible.

No one yet has come along to tell our aging population how large a component relief has become, but Jennifer's research shows how very prevalent the feeling is. For her doctoral dissertation in 1991, she interviewed a group of widows and widowers who had lost spouses to cancer in the previous two years. Although she didn't ask respondents whether they were relieved for their own sake or their loved one's, her findings are revealing. Fully 73.3 percent of the subjects identified relief as one of their primary responses following the death. Even more interestingly, 23 percent said they felt emotions "more intense than relief" and admitted such feelings as "extreme thankfulness," "extreme gratitude," "happiness," "delight," and "peace."

Many today could identify with the Greek hero Tithonus, to whom the gods granted immortality but forgot to include eternal youth. Although he sank into decrepitude, he could not die. At last his wife, Aurora, goddess of the dawn, locked him in a room, where, as author Edith Hamilton tells it, "He babbled endlessly, words with no meaning." Although Greek mythology dates to hundreds of years before Christ, Tithonus's plight has a strangely modern ring, as many who work in the health field could affirm.

"I don't know why some of these patients keep coming back for chemotherapy," a hospice nurse who works at a chemotherapy clinic sighed. "They drag themselves here week after week, and some of them, I don't know how they do it. We've managed to chemically prolong the quantity of life but haven't improved the quality." She believes that pharmaceuticals, especially, are responsible for the extended deaths she sees. "Even twenty years ago, people wouldn't have lived this long—and suffered this long," she told us. "It feels all wrong to me."

Presumably, the patients who stagger in week after week for their chemotherapy treatments want to live. Those being kept alive in hospitals and intensive-care units are frequently there against their wills—literally. "Advance directives," or living wills, set down on paper a person's instructions regarding end-of-life care. If you don't want to be given CPR or put on a respirator if your chances of recovery from an accident or illness are slim, you make out one of these documents and hope that it is followed when the time comes. However, the results of a multimillion-dollar study conducted by the Robert Wood Johnson Foundation, a health care foundation, from 1989 to 1991 and from 1992 to 1994, proved "extremely disappointing," according to two nurses who evaluated it. "The major conclusion of this intervention study was that increased efforts to improve communication about patients' preferences for end-of-life care to physicians did not have a significant impact on the care that is provided in hospitals," they wrote. Educated as well as socialized to preserve life at all costs, physicians were reluctant to write "do not resuscitate" orders despite patient requests, the authors concluded.

American medicine has determined that death is the enemy and often enlists every remedy, no matter the age or condition of the patient, to keep it at bay—creating a new category of patient that might be termed, in the words of one wife, the "chronically living."

None of us would want to do without the medical advances we have come to take for granted. As mothers, we are intensely glad that such scourges as polio, diphtheria, and whooping cough are now footnotes in the history books. Like mothers throughout America, we can be reasonably certain that the children we gave birth to will see adulthood—unlike those of a century ago, who had large numbers of children in order to see a few survive. And we weren't particularly worried, having our babies in the 1970s and 1980s, of dying of postpartum infection. In the dentist's chair, or on the operating table, we're fervently grateful for the benefits of modern pain control.

However, these blessings have come at a high price. At the turn of the century, death was sudden and swift. Women died, within hours, while giving birth; often their babies did, too. Farm accidents claimed many. Acute illnesses and infections, for which there were no antibiotics, killed within days. With the exception of tuberculosis, prolonged death was unusual. With our increasing knowledge of human physiology, the picture has changed. Pneumonia, "the old man's friend," which carried off those with injuries and illnesses in earlier times, and did so fairly painlessly, can now be cured—sparing the patient for a more painful end. In nursing school, Jennifer heard stories, apocryphal, she hoped, about elderly patients being kept waiting for a long time in hallways outside the X-ray department (always chilly because the equipment must be kept at low temperatures) in the hope that they would catch pneumonia.

Superbugs have driven the development of superdrugs. Sophisticated medical technology such as pacemakers, kidney dialysis, feeding tubes, respirators, and portable oxygen tanks are widely available, and many of the lucky recipients of these marvels will be doomed to extended life spans. The medical gods have decreed that we can live forever, locked in a room, babbling endlessly.

Many times, cancer, previously a death sentence, becomes chronic rather than acute. An initial surgery leads to a second and third and fourth, as the patient waits in dread for a recurrence. Will another round of chemotherapy or radiation bring about the desired remission? Will a bone marrow transplant? Or will these slash/burn/poison measures only diminish the quality of life? Loved ones wait and worry right alongside the patient. There's a joke making the rounds that goes, "Why are there nails on coffins?" "Answer: So an oncologist won't order another round of chemotherapy." Even AIDS, one of the few communicable illnesses in recent times to spell certain death, has been transmuted into a chronic illness by means of drugs, and risky sex is again on the rise.

Dick Dolan and his wife, Lucile, experienced the kind of long dying that is becoming routine these days. Dick and Lucile grew up in the same small town on the plains of central Montana, surrounded by wheat fields stretching to the horizon. Dick's family had a long history of diabetes, and he developed it in his fifties. One day, according to Lucile, he went into the bathroom and "everything was blood." The doctor told them there could be only one reason for that much blood: cancer. However, after numerous bladder tumors were removed, and rounds of chemotherapy completed, Dick's doctor assured him that he'd never had this type of cancer recur. But Dick's did, necessitating the removal of his bladder, then one of his kidneys. One of the most difficult things for Lucile was watching her husband do everything right—he was a model patient, whether it came to his diabetes care or his cancer appointments—yet still get worse. When he noticed blood in his urine again, he guessed it was the cancer invading the remaining kidney. He was right. "The cancer wasn't painful," Lucile remembers, "but the procedures were."

Dick became weaker. "He was very vital," Lucile says. "He loved hunting and baseball. He played football in high school and was still very active." His decline, she says, "was hard to watch." During surgery on the remaining kidney, the doctor presented Lucile with a choice no wife should have to make. He could remove the kidney and Dick would need dialysis, or leave the kidney and Dick would have a bit more quality of life. The couple owned a small cabin in the tiny winter resort town of Lincoln, Montana, and Dick had always dreamed of living there permanently, where he could watch the deer and elk that came right into the yard. However, the cabin depended on a generator for electricity, and Dick's doctor vetoed using it for home dialysis. Lucile agonized but opted to let Dick keep the kidney, even though it meant fewer months of life.

Dick was lucky in a way; he died at the cabin he loved. "He had a pouch made out of his intestine he urinated into, because they had removed his bladder. He had a Hickman catheter, because his veins were so thin and collapsed. We had to put his IV tubes through that, and it was a worry," says Lucile. "We knew every wide spot in the road," she remembers, "so that he could go to the bathroom." Her eyes fill. "Seeing this big, strong, capable man have to use those things. . . ." Although she misses him every day, she says, "I don't miss seeing how emaciated he was, covered with scars, not knowing what the worst was going to be." She is still angry at the unfairness of his ordeal. "The thing that bothers me is, he did everything they told him, and everything they said wouldn't happen, happened."

The hospice movement has been a boon to an aging nation for many reasons, not the least of which is its enlightened attitude toward pain control. It seems incredible, not to mention scandalous, that chronic pain, despite all our medical sophistication, is a continuing problem for many and presents a powerful obstacle to peaceful dying. Pain saps energy and changes personalities. It robs the patient of restful sleep, so that the world always looks gray. It leads to apathy because it kills the hope that things will ever get better. Unrelenting pain can lead to thoughts of suicide and is the driving force behind recent assisted suicide legislation. Public opinion surveys show that most Americans are more afraid of pain than death—and with good reason: A 1995 study by the Robert Wood Johnson Foundation found that half of all dying patients suffer moderate to severe pain. Unfortunately, according to a recent report by AARP, most doctors have never had any education in pain control. Pain-killing drugs carry stigma, and doctors are still reluctant to prescribe them. Narcotics depress breathing, and doses strong enough to kill the pain can also kill the patient. And one still hears statements like "she might become addicted," even though the patient is only days or weeks from death.

As a hospice nurse reflects, "We can alleviate pain, but not suffering." And whereas pain is physical—and therefore theoretically within reach of intervention—suffering is psychological, and the suffering accompanying terminal illness can seem endless. Having to be turned frequently because every bone protrudes; losing any shred of dignity due to incontinence; not being able to eat; being unable to sleep when your family caregiver longs to be asleep like the rest of the world; watching your nest egg dwindle because of the costs of medical care; these are only some of the ways sick people and their families suffer.

Suffering can follow losses both obvious and subtle, such as the series of "ambiguous losses" that accompanies extended illness. Because they aren't apparent to anyone outside the immediate family, these losses may be met with skepticism and dismissal. However, Chris found they were the most difficult thing about living with multiple sclerosis (MS)—both the uncertainty they brought, as well as the impossibility of grieving them fully. While to the family a serious diagnosis means the death of many dreams, the patient may still look and act well. A wife who acts grief-stricken may be told to buck up, there are lots of medicines available, and what about bee venom, by the way? Then come the other losses: loss of ambulation; loss of ability to feed oneself; loss of sexual potency; loss of being able to concentrate on anything but one's own discomfort; loss of mental acuity. Placing someone in a nursing home is a wrenching loss, but it is not seen as "big enough" to grieve and thus receives little acknowledgment or support. Yet Chris found it was more difficult than Don's actual death five years later. Each loss takes the patient another step further outside the family system, and by the time he stops breathing the family has long since psychologically buried him.

Adele Bachmann, whose mother was seriously handicapped by a brain injury that resulted from a bungled surgery, says that her mother often "practiced dying"—to the terror of her family. On one outing, Adele, her mother, and Adele's niece had taken a tour boat to a remote island. The boat delivered passengers, then returned for them an hour later. Suddenly, Adele's mother "just pitched forward onto the sand," says Adele. "I caught her before she hit the ground, but she had lost consciousness. My niece absolutely freaked out, she was just beside herself, saying she would never take the tour boat again." For Adele, the whole scene was surreal. "Here's my mom dying, and we have to wait for the tour boat." Her mother revived before the boat came, but all three were shaken. "Anticipatory grief, there were so many times," Adele says. "She went through hell, and we went with her."

When her forty-seven-year-old husband began acting strangely, Jessie Randolph didn't know what to think. "He began to stare out the window for hours," she recalls, "and he lost simple, logical reasoning tasks." Although the New York Yankees won the first four games of the World Series that year, making them world champions, Jack insisted there were three more games to go—and no amount of arguing on Jessie's part would convince him otherwise. The Randolphs wouldn't know for another year that Jack had Lou Gehrig's disease (amyotrophic lateral sclerosis), a rare type known as "bulbar onset," in which thinking skills are affected first. "He's, like, going crazy, or getting dumb, and there was nobody to talk to," Jessie says, remembering the anguished uncertainty of that time. "That was worse than when he died." By the time of his actual death, she wondered at her lack of tears. "I thought, here I've lost my husband, and I should be sadder than this, I should be crying. Then I thought, no, Jessie, you cried when you lost him, a year ago, you cried lots then."

No wonder that, more and more often, death is welcomed. Donna Bueti, a hospice nurse, has had plenty of opportunities to study the behavior of hospice families in

her seven years on the job. A keen observer of human nature, she says that frequently, in the days before a death,
families seem disconnected. "You're giving them instructions about medications, and they don't seem to get it, so
you're writing them down. And you can see they're just
overwhelmed." Once death occurs, though, a dramatic
change takes place. "You see them mobilize. It's a kind of
quickness. After a death, they say, we need to do this and
do that." She suspects that "even as a way of getting
through the death beforehand, I bet they thought about
all this. It's all planned out, they know just what they
need to do, and there's some relief."

Alternately, she notices a kind of slowness. "I've been
watching them being tense and tight, but now they're sitting back in a chair, and their shoulders are down, and
there's a calmness. It's like having finished something."
She attempts to frame her observations in words for the
benefit of these families. "I say, 'There must be some relief
now.' And just see what happens. And it's a floodgate, because that's a disenfranchised emotion for a lot of people.
Family members respond with comments like 'He's in
such a better place' or 'Now we can remember who she
was before the illness.'"

Donna sees her job partly as one of enabling people to
identify feelings, a technique she believes finds more re-
ceptiveness among hospice families. "I've been involved a
few times with non-hospice patients," she says, "and I've
said, 'Oh, you must be relieved,' and they look at me like,
'I can't believe what I just heard.' I get funny looks, oh
yeah." Speculating that because the hospice environment
offers so much safety ("You've seen them at their worst"),

she often sees gratitude when she helps people do this, because they come to see that these responses are normal and even desirable. "Sometimes after a death, the family will be laughing and talking, and one of them will say, 'You must think we're a weird family,' and I say no, not at all. There's a great deal of happiness, and they've stayed with the process to the end, and now [the family member] is comfortable and on the other shore."

Stephanie Kellogg helped her mother to that other shore. Sixty-nine when her husband died, the plucky older woman embarked on a new life, traveling and taking classes in academic subjects as well as piano lessons. At age seventy-five, only a week after cataract surgery, mother and daughter took a fifteen-mile hike through Montana's rugged Absaroka Mountains. Stephanie recalls fondly, "We ran into some people on the trail who commented that they had met some fifty-year-olds who were hiking, and my mother just giggled. She didn't want them to know how old she was."

On Memorial Day 1998, while sunning herself in a backyard hammock, Stephanie's mom had a stroke. While recovering, she had another, this time losing control of her eyelids and one of her legs. One of the eyelids eventually opened properly, but the other didn't. "So she was a one-eyed mother after that," says Stephanie. For the next four years, Stephanie's mom was in and out of nursing homes as she worked toward being able to live alone. She became depressed there, says the younger woman. "It was so disturbing there, the noise, the interruptions, the lack of privacy. And her room was right by the main door, so every time anyone went by they could look in and see. She said that she was starting to think that this was what the world was really all about, people screaming, emergency things going on. And she didn't want to associate with anyone there because she was not one of those 'senior citizens.'"

Seeing her still alert mother confined to a place like that wrung Stephanie's heart, especially because her body was gradually becoming a prison, too. "She slowly lost her independence, lost her hearing, she was losing her sight to diabetes, she couldn't walk by herself . . . her freedoms were taken away from her." Yet her mother dealt with these losses with surprising aplomb. She still prized visits from her children, Stephanie and her two brothers, cherishing such things as back rubs and having lotion applied to her skin.

Eventually, Stephanie quit her job to be more available to her mother, who was once more living in her own home with the help of attendants. While transferring her to a chair, one of her sons heard a soft pop, and she groaned as if something had ruptured. She stopped eating and her stomach began to swell—with blood, the family guessed.

By the time Stephanie arrived, her mother was in a coma. Stephanie's two brothers, panicked, wanted to put her back in the nursing home, but Stephanie asked them to wait. They were only too glad to turn their mother's care over to her. Stephanie longed for one last chance to say good-bye. "I couldn't connect with her," she says. "At first, I thought she was squeezing my hand, but then I realized it was just a reflex." She wanted badly to revive her mother somehow but recognized this as a selfish impulse. "I wanted to take her to the hospital, and get fluids into her, but I knew that I couldn't. Because it was just the process of dying and I had to let her go through it." Courageously, she decided to accompany her mother on her final journey.

Although she was tempted to call for help "Because," she says, "I had no clue what to do for her, or how to keep her comfortable. I kept her lips wet," she feared interference by the medical establishment, who might put her mother in the hospital. "She had a living will, and I knew she didn't want to be revived," she says. By Monday morning she knew she could see it through and that this was what her mother needed her to do. Then the home health aide arrived. Stephanie remembers, "She went into the bedroom with me where Mom was, and just freaked out and was screaming at my mother, 'We've got to get fluids back into you, we have to get you back up.' I took her out of the room and sat her down at the kitchen table and told her that Mom was dying and we just had to let it happen." Her mother chose that moment to die. "When I went back in after a few minutes, she had died. She was a wise woman."

Stephanie lay down beside her mother and cried, hard, for an hour. "I felt so empty at that point, but I couldn't wish her back, I wouldn't have done it for the world. She had deteriorated to a point where there would be no way of recovery. I told her, I don't think you're ever going to recover from this, so, Mom, the first opportunity you find to go, take it. Fly away."

Sometimes, in this age of medical marvels, saying no is the most difficult choice of all. The mere fact that the elaborate life-saving equipment exists—dialysis in Dick

Dolan's case, intravenous fluids and maybe "life-saving" surgery in Stephanie's mother's—carries the implication that it should be used; the fact of its existence makes it seem necessary as well, and not using it is somehow morally wrong. Respecting the wishes of the dying, as Lucile and Stephanie discovered, can be the hardest choice— as well as the kindest. As difficult as it was, Stephanie was able to be midwife to her mother's passage out of life. She found the strength to give her mother that most precious of all gifts: a peaceful death.

Chuck Noble had every reason to feel relieved for himself when his father died, but instead he felt relief for the unfortunate older man. Lloyd Noble died on October 23, 2000, but according to Chuck, his death occurred long before then—fifty years earlier, in fact. "He was a victim of World War II. I say 'victim' because he was in World War II and was never all right after that." According to Chuck, Lloyd's brother was killed in action, and Lloyd was sent to R&R in Hawaii. While there, he was kicked in the head by a horse, after which he began having bad dreams. "He was one of the first people to go into Hiroshima after they dropped the A-bomb," says Chuck, "and he had to go in and bulldoze dead bodies. Some of the stuff he did would've put most people over the edge years ago."

In 1957 Chuck's parents divorced, and he and his two older siblings went to live with their dad. Three years later, apparently in the grip of a delusion, Lloyd shot and killed Chuck's mother. "I was really bitter for a lot of years," Chuck says. "Mom was my favorite." Lloyd was sentenced to prison, and young Chuck was left in the care of an aunt. Many years later, in his twenties, he went to the Montana State Hospital at Warm Springs and asked to see his dad's records. The hospital refused, so he returned with a court order. For the first time, Chuck realized his dad's illness had a name: paranoid schizophrenia. He began to feel empathy for the man he had avoided most of his life and arranged to see his dad—now released from prison—more often, driving him to appointments at the veterans hospital and inviting him to his home for family occasions. When Lloyd violated parole he was sent back to prison and, when released again, fell in and out of jobs and living situations. He took twenty-five to thirty pills a day to control his mental and physical ailments, but the bars he visited in search of company didn't help him stay on his medication. "When he was normal (in other words, taking his medication) he was the best person you could know," says Chuck. Chuck began to see firsthand the unremitting hell of mental illness. "His life was a series of hospitalizations and incarcerations," he says. Sometimes Lloyd talked about a civilization that existed six feet underground, or he told Chuck he could go to Mars whenever he wanted. Once he told Chuck not to touch pennies because they were radioactive. Chuck's choice of words when he talks about the past reflects his compassion for his father: He speaks of his mother's murder as "the incident" or "the accident," never "the murder." Eventually Lloyd died of a ruptured blood vessel at the veterans hospital where he had spent so much time, and Chuck was relieved that his dad was out of his tormented life, as well as sad for himself. "There was sadness, but I felt good because he was such a troubled person and he didn't have to deal with it anymore. He had his own demons," he says. Far from resenting the caregiving role he had played, Chuck felt empty. "It was a long winter for me," he acknowledges.

Lucile and Stephanie were haunted in large part by what their loved ones used to be; images of the active, athletic husband and the curious, vital mother contributed to their suffering—and consequent relief. In contrast, Chuck Noble saw the terrible gestalt of schizophrenia and was relieved that his father's demons were vanquished.

Suffering can also be projected, as Thane and Kathy Brandt discovered. The parents of a toddler son, Zachary, the Brandts were delighted when Kathy conceived again. At the routine twenty-week ultrasound, Kathy felt a special urgency. "Please make sure everything's all right," she said to the technician. "I had a bad dream last week that something was wrong." Clutching Thane's hand, she watched the wavering images on the screen as their unborn baby's every organ was examined. His heart was last. Thane, who worked in the X-ray department, noticed immediately that something didn't look right. "What's that white mass?" he asked the technician. "You need to go get Dr. Olds," they were told. Kathy, suddenly in a panic, tried to pray but couldn't remember the words. Their small hospital referred them to one with a pediatric cardiologist, who diagnosed their baby with hypoplastic left heart syndrome. "Basically, the heart doesn't develop," says Kathy. "We had two chambers that were perfect, but the left side didn't work." The doctor assured her that she was not to blame; the baby's heart had probably stopped developing before she even realized she was pregnant. The baby, a boy they now called Matthew, would die soon after birth unless he was whisked immediately into the operating room.

There, he would have surgery to turn his four-chamber heart into a two-chamber one until the next big step: a heart transplant.

The Brandts turned to the Internet for information and began to doubt their options. The costs—financial, emotional, and physical—seemed huge. Infant hearts were in short supply. One couple they heard about, says Kathy, "decided to do a transplant, they'd given the baby some kind of drug to keep a duct open that closes after birth, and he died at three weeks, waiting for a heart. They never got to hold him, never got to spend quality time with him." To her, that wasn't acceptable. "I wanted to hold Matthew. I wanted to be sure he died in my arms, and I didn't want him to have any pain and suffering." Above all, she tried to keep in mind what was good for Matthew by putting herself in his place. "I struggled at first, but then I realized I couldn't do it to a brand new baby, put him through open heart surgery, and a heart transplant. I couldn't." One of the couple's worst moments was watching Matthew kick and yawn and suck his fist on the ultrasound; immediately after, they headed to the mortuary to plan his funeral. The irony of their situation was overwhelming to Kathy. "I said to Thane, 'We should be planning his life. We shouldn't be going to the funeral home.' I felt like I was letting him down, like we were just giving up."

As her belly grew, so did her dread. "I was terrified to have him, not because I didn't want to meet him, but I just knew it would make it harder to say good-bye. For the most part, these babies die peacefully, but they do have a difficult time breathing, and they do have some fluid retention because their kidneys are starting to fail, and I was very scared to watch my baby die. I was afraid he was going to suffer."

Matthew lived two and a half hours, and Kathy describes it, her voice full of wonder, as "the most fulfilling day of my life." She explains, "I was just holding this baby and praying he was going to die peacefully, and he did." Matthew's aorta turned out to be so underdeveloped that a transplant would have been impossible. "So after all that worry and stress of all those months, that question was taken away from me, which I am really thankful for," she says. "It was a huge gift, because I don't ever have to think, what if?"

In the days that followed, she felt overwhelmingly relieved and peaceful—and guilty, when she saw Thane struggle with feelings of anger and bitterness. She realized she had grieved for Matthew for nine months because she had carried him, but Thane had been able to postpone his grief. And though she will always wonder who Matthew might have become, and mourn that she will never know, Kathy reflects, "It's funny, because, on my really bad days, I sometimes make jokes, when Zach's having a bad day, or Thane and I are at each other's throats, I say 'I think we miss Matthew more than he misses us.' Because life can be stressful. I think of him in heaven, and happy."

In these stories, we clearly see overwhelming sadness. But there is also hope. For these people, death was not the enemy but rather an event that brought redemption to a life troubled by physical illness, mental illness, or serious disability. They have come to see it as a gift and have integrated it into the spectrum of life. As Kathy Brandt noted, "It's like I have a new relationship with death. I don't view it as that awful, terrible, ugly thing no one wants to talk about anymore. I view it as part of what everybody has to do."

3

Dual Relief

"Here lie the remains of John Hall, Grocer. The world is not worth a fig, and I have good raisins for saying so."
—Epitaph in Dunmore, Ireland

Chris's story:

When Don died, I was overwhelmed with relief. As I walked into his tiny cell at the nursing home to retrieve his belongings, just hours after his death, the first thing I saw was the big, black, ugly electric wheelchair that had come to seem like part of his body. I fell to my knees and put my arms around it, sobbing. "At least," I told him, "you're free of this wretched thing you depended on for so long, this hated travesty of the freedom you should have had as a vigorous young man. I'd wish you back in a minute," I wept, "but not the way you were. Never the way you were. You're no longer in the grip of this vicious disease. Donnie," I wept, "you're finally free."

In the summer of 1978, everything seemed to be going our way. Don and I had been college sweethearts who had married in 1972. By that fateful summer, we had two healthy children, a daughter, four, and a son, eighteen months. The previous summer we had moved back to Montana, where our families lived, and Don had started a new job as an insurance underwriter for a branch of a big insurance company. One warm summer afternoon, he came home from a fishing trip complaining that his legs "felt funny." He said that while he had been tramping the brushy banks of a local creek, fly-fishing, his legs had felt wobbly. He "couldn't feel them" for a few seconds, he said. The episode was over quickly, though, and we dismissed it from our minds.

Soon, however, it was apparent something was seriously wrong. Don's balance was unreliable, and when he tried to start a jogging regime, thinking he was just out of shape, he stumbled and fell. By the end of an agonizing year (in those days, there weren't any conclusive diagnostic tools), we had a pretty good idea that he had MS.

We prayed that it would take a benign course—from our reading we knew that this mysterious illness took all kinds of different forms—but within a year he needed a walker, and two years later, a wheelchair.

I took over driving him to and from work, and, thankfully, his desk was only twenty feet from the front entrance, which had no steps. But gradually, his speech became harder to understand, his upper body strength faded, and he couldn't hold a telephone to his ear. He began to have bowel and bladder accidents.

Ten years after his diagnosis, he finally had to retire. Now that he was home all day, I was responsible for all his care, and after his forced retirement, which devastated him emotionally, he became even weaker. The kids and I took turns lifting his head from his chest so he could see. That fall, he agreed to enter a nursing home. Our family doctor believed he would die within a year.

Placing Don in a nursing home at the age of forty-one was in some ways a more painful death than his physical death five years later. It pitched me headlong into the bleakest patch of loneliness I'd ever known. I didn't know how to live. Was I wife or widow? I was dealing with an "ambiguous loss" of the worst kind, a sort of life-in-death. I knew Don would not emerge alive from that place, because I knew the enemy too well. MS was not something one rehabilitated from.

At that point I thought I could see the end of the trail—and it was not an unwelcome sight. But surprisingly, Don stabilized in the nursing home and lived another five years there. I brought him home on Sundays so that he could catch up with the kids, now young teenagers, and so we could eat dinner as a family. One of those afternoons I accidentally broke his hip as I was transferring him from the wheelchair to our bed. At the time, it seemed like a minor bump. No one had warned me that after so many years of inactivity his bones were as fragile as old china.

Our doctor, unwilling to put him through the rigors of major surgery, advised waiting for the bone to heal, but Don was in pain and wanted to have the hip replaced. A few weeks after the hours-long surgery, he developed a postsurgical infection, which led to pneumonia. He died peacefully one Sunday in February 1993.

I could hardly believe that his suffering was over at last. He had had so many infections over the years, one time a bladder infection bad enough to cause bloody urine, as well as several bouts of pneumonia, that I had a hard time grasping the fact that this time he was really dead. It had been so painful watching this good man go through so many years of unrelenting suffering. The illness couldn't do any more to him; finally he was out of reach.

And I was free. The end of his suffering meant, to a large degree, the end of mine, too. And I felt free in other ways—free to move on with other relationships; free of the financial worries that had gone along with his illness; free to make decisions concerning my own future. Even the freedom to grieve this final loss felt liberating, since there had been so many losses leading up to this final one. When you know the latest loss is not the last, you live in a constant state of alert. It's like walking around with your arms over your head, waiting for the next brick to fall.

It's probably a natural tendency—a very human one—to look ahead to the future so that losing someone you love so much hurts less. After Don went to the nursing home, about five years before he died, I joined a group for divorced, widowed, and separated Catholics (over Don's protests) and began to make single friends. I began to build a writing career. During these years, I learned to make decisions regarding the house, the yard, and the kids. I bought a car alone for the first time and arranged the financing. Inevitably, I began to think of myself as a single person.

But I couldn't have it both ways. Directing energy toward the future meant that I spent less energy, both emotional and physical, on my husband. To this day, I wish I had been more present during his last weeks. Not that I stopped visiting completely; I was still at the nursing home several times a week. But now I can think of so many ways I could have eased his dying.

I was angry and confused when he decided to have hip replacement surgery, because he seemed far too debilitated to survive such a serious operation. And I was right; within a few weeks he developed a postsurgical infection, and his lungs were too weak to fight the pneumonia that followed. The children and I were with him when he took his last breath, holding him and talking to him and loving him, but I'll always regret that his last few weeks were shadowed with anger and misunderstanding.

Chris experienced "dual relief," that is, relief for herself as well as for her husband. The relief she felt for Don was readily understandable to her close friends and family; fewer would have been willing to listen to her relief for herself. Yet these are logical reactions when the illness has been long and severe. Those most likely to feel dual relief are caregivers, though this is not always the case.

Even when pain is managed adequately and the dying person's personality remains more or less intact, the stress of caregiving—and as any caregiver will tell you, the psychological toll is at least as onerous as the physical—will prove a heavy burden. When the chronically ill one is a beloved spouse or partner, as in Chris's case, the steady loss of function, and the sense of helplessness to do anything about it, is nearly unbearable; no sooner is one loss grieved than another one looms. At this point, the biggest challenge facing family members is how to stay present to the person while disengaging emotionally. This is a difficult task—maybe impossible.

While the tremendous relief that occurs after the end of a prolonged illness is partly the result of having grieved the person so intensely prior to death, it may also be facilitated by the emotional detaching that took place then. Family members recognize that the person they loved has been missing from their lives for a long time, and when death comes, it will be welcomed rather than dreaded.

Fletcher Newby, seventy-five, knows these feelings. Years earlier, he was leaning against a wall at a college mixer when Elaine Crowe walked in, presenting, to Fletcher's mind, "a vision of loveliness." For him, it was love at first sight. "I'm not sure I knocked anybody down, but I intended to be there first," he recalls. They were engaged within two weeks and married within three months.

But their bliss was not to last. At twenty-six, the willowy Elaine, who was sometimes mistaken for a model, was diagnosed with rheumatoid arthritis (RA). For the next forty-six years she endured the ravages of RA—the fractures, deformity, joint replacements, and pain—as

Fletcher took over more and more of the "housekeeping and groundskeeping." A wildlife biologist who specialized in wolverines, Fletcher didn't mind the outdoor work, but he disliked the cleaning and cooking. Gradually, Fletcher became her full-time nurse, too. At age seventy-one, Elaine developed breathing problems, her lungs having been weakened by all the steroids she had taken for the arthritis. "Medicare got tougher and tougher about home health payments, so we didn't have much," he says. So he was the one who set up and maintained Elaine's CPAP machine (continuous positive airway pressure), which monitored her breathing at night. "I didn't have to do diapers, but I suppose you know what a suppository is?" he asks. "Even the nurses were surprised I would do that," he admits. "But I'm a biologist, so I'm more knowledgeable than someone else might have been. And she was so grateful. It made a difference, absolutely."

Then Elaine contracted one of the flu strains not contained in the vaccine, and the harsh cough she developed ruptured an artery in her lower back. The artery was a small one but caused significant bleeding, and she needed several transfusions. Her surgeon wanted to inject her kidneys with dye in order to pinpoint it and cauterize it, but the dye would cause enough kidney damage that Elaine would henceforth have to be on dialysis. So in addition to her other problems, she would have a physician-induced one as well. Fletcher and Elaine had seen this moment coming, and they had discussed it at length— many times. He refused to put his wife through any more suffering. With their three adult children at the bedside,

Elaine's life support was removed. Then, he recalls, "she just faded away." He held her hand till it got cold.

Overcome with grief, Fletcher was nevertheless aware of his new freedom. "A great burden has been relieved from me, but a great loneliness has settled on me," he announced to his children. In his mind, the two strangely balanced each other. Watching Elaine wither had been devastating for Fletcher, who never lost the initial ardor he felt at the sight of her so many years earlier. And despite her pain and physical limitations, Elaine had been a generous companion. "By a burden being lifted, I mean the burden of caregiving, the burden of disease. Watching this woman succumb, that's what I mean," he says. And, he reflects, "I had had enough of doing two jobs."

He looked for ways to ease his grief. He bought a portable tape deck and played their song, "Always," over and over, weeping. He also wrote Elaine a good-bye letter. On the second anniversary of her death, he felt ready to put the past behind him. He started a consulting business and, through it, met a woman one month younger than his own daughter and remarried. Elaine, who knew he would outlive her, had encouraged him many times to remarry after she died. In fact, Fletcher wonders "if she didn't arrange my marriage to Pam." Maybe, he thinks, it's Elaine's way of showing her gratitude for all he did for her.

At present, our understanding and ability to deal with the mental deterioration that inevitably goes along with aging and illness lag far behind our ability to motivate mere flesh. The etiology of mental and behavioral changes is not well understood, and depression, anger, withdrawal, even violence, will throw a nasty kink into the already difficult task of caregiving. Andrew Solomon, author of *The Noonday Demon: An Atlas of Depression*, suggests that depression among the elderly may be much more widespread than previously suspected.

Although there are many contenders for world's cruelest disease, Alzheimer's ranks right up there, cunningly turning brilliant, capable adults into babies, and petulant babies at that. Hospice nurse Donna Bueti told us, "I recently had a patient whose husband had Alzheimer's, and she said he wasn't in any pain, but she suffered right along with him, the indignities. And I do think, more than any other kind of death, family members of people with Alzheimer's experience massive relief." A woman we interviewed observed, "I lost my mother twice, once to Alzheimer's, and once to death." Families end up caring for the husk of the person they knew until death comes, sometimes as long as eight or ten years. Often, they mourn two deaths.

Dick Appling's wife, Marijane, inherited the "family curse" of Alzheimer's in her late sixties. "Her mother had Alzheimer's, so we were pretty sure it would come to her, and we watched for it," he says. Seeing it coming didn't make it any easier to deal with; if anything, it was harder. One thing Dick had always prized about Marijane was her quick mind. When they were high school students in Eugene, Oregon, she had put her books in his locker, then feigned surprise when he pointed out the error. Later, she confessed that she had done it on purpose—she was tall, and he was one of the few boys she didn't tower over. She was a shrewd bridge partner, managed the household budgeting, and picked stocks with considerable skill.

"She bought carpet stock one year, because the weather was terrible, and there were floods all over the country, and she said carpets are going to be needed," Dick says. Come April 1 of each year, Dick was on his guard, because Marijane, "a frivolous, fun-loving imp," always devised a way to make him into a fool. Try as he might, he was never able to outwit her. His job as a mining engineer often took him to remote places, so in the summers she would pack up their two kids and join him. They camped out, first in a tent and, when they became more affluent, a trailer, making his work assignments, for at least part of the year, feel like an extended picnic. Besides having a fun-loving nature, Marijane was "classy and well-groomed," a woman who took pride in her appearance and always decorated the house for holidays.

But gradually Alzheimer's stole each endearing trait. She began wearing the same clothes for days on end—and sleeping in them, too. She wouldn't bathe, and when he asked her to, she got angry. One day, as they strolled in the mall, she saw a pantsuit in a store window and bought it. Dick was pleased—until she began sleeping in it, then bought a new skirt and put that on over the pantsuit. She stopped combing her hair and resisted his suggestions that she wash it, so he conspired with her hairdresser to call her Friday afternoons and suggest she come in for a shampoo and set. Marijane would agree to these "spontaneous" suggestions, and Dick's heart lifted at the sight of his freshly coifed wife.

The darker aspects of her illness were impossible to circumvent. To Dick's despair, Marijane, realizing that her mind was beginning to desert her, and with memories of her mother's ordeal still vivid, begged him to help her kill herself. "I don't want to be here! I should die!" she'd rage. With tears in his eyes, he refused. "I'll help you with anything else, but I can't do that." He read of a lawyer in Spokane whose case touched him. "He cared for his wife at home," Dick says. "She was much more advanced than Marijane, in a wheelchair. And finally, he picked up a pistol and shot her in the back of head. He said, 'Good-bye, Doris,' and pulled the trigger. I knew that society condemned him, but I knew the stress he was under, and I knew that I was sympathetic."

As Marijane's illness deepened she became more combative, sometimes running away across the fields that surrounded the neighborhood. At first he ran after her and tried to reason with her. "What's wrong?" he implored. "You know!" she spat. But he didn't. Eventually he would follow her from a distance in the car, checking her progress with field glasses in case she got too close to the nearby highway.

He put Marijane in a nursing home, and she seemed happier. But his real deliverance came in the form of a deadly disease. "One morning, she collapsed, and after the collapse, we found out it was from lack of oxygen and dehydration." The long minutes of oxygen deprivation turned the tiger into a house cat. "It glossed over the worst stages of the Alzheimer's," he says. "She just sat and watched things, smiled her smile. It wasn't the hell the previous months had been." Marijane's collapse, it turned out, had been caused by a blood clot from the lung—the result of lung cancer that had gone undetected.

Marijane's end, a few months later, was surprisingly swift and peaceful. "She'd had dinner at the home's dining room, and the nurse took her back to her room, and when the nurse noticed she was having a little trouble breathing, they called me. I was there within twelve minutes, and by then, she was gone." He had never expected that cancer would be a blessing, but "she had no pain. I was so grateful for it." It was the most crushing of ironies that modern medicine was of no help with her devastating disease, but cancer was. Marijane's death presented Dick with an array of conflicting emotions. "When she died, I was so glad, and I was so sad. I didn't know which I was, sad or glad. I knew that her death spared her pain, but at the same time, I was perfectly happy to go on caring for her in that nursing home, if she could still be there." He couldn't sort it out. "You know, nothing is ever that straightforward and simple. I wouldn't want her back for a minute, if she was going to be the way she was when she left. If I could bring her back the way she was twenty years ago, yes, I would have done it."

He remembered the agonizing moments when she would beg him to help her die, and although he would have done anything for her, he could not cross that barrier. "She was so abject, she hurt so badly, not physically, but mentally she hurt so badly. She was a proud woman, I don't know another way to put it, she was simply a proud woman, and she saw how she had become."

She dealt with the physical signs of aging gracefully, he says. "She'd been an outdoor girl, and she'd been in the sun a lot, and her face was wrinkled. She was beautiful to me, and she was distressed over her wrinkles, but she'd come to grips with that years ago." The mental changes were another story. "One time, she was loading the dishwasher, and she stumbled, and she fell, and it just triggered it. She lay there and cried, 'I want to die, I want to die'. . . That was hell for me, at that time. There's no way you can describe that. I'd have to listen to this, and tell her, 'I can't help you, I can't do it for you.' And so it was a very sick feeling to me." At last, he reflected, Marijane had her wish.

Norma Imber's response following the death of her husband Robert was much less complicated. "If anyone whose spouse has been sick tells you there's no relief, don't believe them," she says flatly.

When the phone call came, Norma couldn't believe that her husband, Robert, was really dead. "I thought, *This can't be true, he's playing possum,*" she says. She couldn't grasp the fact that this would be her last trip to the nursing home. "Here's me, I had been going for ten years," she says. "I got up every day and went to the nursing home just like people go to work, except no paycheck." Robert had been a great tease, and she was sure he must be playing another joke. Approaching his still body, she remembers, "I kissed him on the forehead to see if he was cold. He was cool but not cold. I picked his eyelids open, looked up his nose, opened his mouth. The kids watched me like I was crazy." She wonders now what they were thinking, although she's never asked them. "It's dreamlike, it's like you're in another place, because death is so mysterious, secretive, suspicious, all those mystical things." Still not convinced, she performed the same comic examination on Robert two more times. "I was finally convinced he wasn't going to open his eyes and say 'Gotcha!'" she says.

During the time Robert had been in the nursing home, Norma had become accustomed to living as a widow, even though, strictly speaking, she was not. This helped her adjustment after Robert's death enormously. Soon after Robert went to the nursing home, she joined National Well Spouses, an organization for those whose spouses have a chronic, severe illness. Eventually she served on the board of directors and facilitated numerous Well Spouse support groups, in the process creating a strong support system. She recalls, "I never felt empty in the days afterward, because of all the wonderful people and the support from Well Spouses especially."

Being a well spouse, whether you join a group or not, puts you in a select club, one with its own special language and humor. Here, wishing a spouse would die is not taboo. Everyone understands. Norma's friend Lois's husband has had MS for twenty years and has been in a nursing home for the past five. "Every time I called Lois to tell her that one of our friends had lost their ill spouse, she'd say, 'Always a bridesmaid, never a bride,'" says Norma. "Then we'd laugh. Sometimes, after visiting her husband in the hospital, she'd call me and say, 'I can smell the flowers!'" As those with ill spouses know, black humor can be sanity-saving, and it doesn't reflect on the love that exists between the couple.

And just because positive reactions are involved doesn't mean that recovering from a death like Don's, Elaine's, Marijane's, or Robert's is easy. Dick Appling's experience, especially, shows that the feelings following a death like this are by no means simple. Just because it has been anticipated, even longed for, doesn't necessarily make it easier to grieve. Therese Rando states that any illness lasting more than eighteen months predisposes to complicated grief. How much more complicated must be the reactions that follow an eighteen-year illness—or, as in Fletcher Newby's case, a forty-six-year one! Rando theorizes that emotional conflict occurs because death approaches and recedes so many times, and because the family both wishes it and dreads it, they are likely to feel guilty when it finally comes.

The large study undertaken by the Institute for Social Research at the the University of Michigan (Changing Lives of Older Couples) bears out Rando's theory. Because longitudinal studies are expensive and time-consuming, few have been done in the area of bereavement. The results of the CLOC study are particularly valuable, both because of its size and because it is one of the few to analyze the quality of the marital relationship prior to the death of one of the couple. The study has followed 1,532 people since 1987; one of the requirements was that the husband had to be sixty-five or older. The results disprove the old thinking that a sudden death is harder to grieve than one following a lingering illness. Instead, the study found that prolonged forewarning of a death meant increased anxiety levels in the survivor for as long as eighteen months afterward. The researchers confirmed that "chronic (or long-term) stressors, such as caregiving or watching a spouse suffer from a debilitating illness, are believed to be more difficult for psychological adjustment than stressors of shorter duration."

These findings come as no surprise to the rest of us. Chris's sister-in-law, Mary, related sharing her grief with a colleague after Don's death. The man frowned. "But you knew he was going to die, didn't you?" he asked. "Yes," Mary replied, exasperated. "We had to watch him get ready to die, then we had to watch him actually die, and now we have to deal with his death. And your point was . . . ?"

It isn't just the death of someone elderly and suffering that can bring relief. Marla Mabry knew her fourth child, Tiffany, was different. At birth she was floppy and lethargic, with skin tags that looked like extra fingers and toes. Unlike Marla's other babies, Tiffany showed no interest in waking up for feedings, and Marla, breasts aching, would have to wake her. When Tiffany was two months old, the Mabrys took her to a pediatric neurologist at prestigious Vanderbilt University. "She's fine," he announced to the apprehensive parents, pointing out that chromosomal studies had detected no abnormalities. But Marla, a physical therapist who had worked with handicapped children, knew in her bones that something was wrong. "Being a [physical therapist], I was looking for midline things," she says. "And at four months, she wasn't bringing her hands to midline, she wasn't playing with her hands, and her postures were still immature. She wasn't grasping things, either." Marla knew from her three older children that this little girl didn't make consistent eye contact; her focus seemed to shift from one eye to the other. Tormented with doubt—*Was she imagining these things? Could the eminent specialist be wrong?*—she began to dread the developmental milestones. "You know, here it is seven months and she doesn't sit, here she is nine months and doesn't crawl." Time proved her intuition correct.

Isolated in a small town, Marla had nowhere to express her grief regarding her daughter, and Marla's reserved personality would have made her uncomfortable in a support group anyway. Her husband's way of coping was to immerse himself in work, and he was emotionally unavailable to her. As Tiffany's condition became more and more obvious, the couple consulted one specialist after another, all of whom asked the same guilt-laden questions: "What was your pregnancy like? Did you run a fever in your first trimester?"

Still, Tiffany grew into a likable child, cheerful in the face of devastating handicaps. She could walk, precariously, with a walker, but her main mode of transportation was crawling. She could feed herself finger food, and though she made meaningful sounds, she couldn't speak.

At thirteen, the age Tiffany died, Marla suspected that she was having mild seizures, which would explain why sometimes her daughter awakened at night, screaming. Marla knew that the shifting hormone levels of puberty drastically affect the number and severity of seizures, and she worried about her daughter. *What if she has a cardiac arrest during one and the oxygen deprivation leaves her comatose? What if she no longer knows her family? What if she is no longer Tiffany?* Her daughter's quality of life wasn't great, but it could have been a lot worse. "Although she was severely limited, she had preferences," Marla says. "There were things and people she liked; she had a personality. If she lost her personality, I don't know what we would have done."

Tiffany also had scoliosis, a progressive curvature of the spine. To correct it would have meant major surgery and wearing a body cast for a year, and Marla would never have been able to explain to Tiffany the whys and wherefores of her situation. Another thing that kept Marla awake at night was that Tiffany weighed only fifty-two pounds, which made her light enough for Marla to carry around. But Tiffany would grow, and Marla wondered how long she could continue to care for her at home. She knew that not all those who care for the developmentally disabled are good people, and not all caregiving is caring. Certainly no one else could care for her little girl like Marla herself.

The night before she died, Tiffany had vomited after she went to bed, as she sometimes did during a seizure. As always, Marla cleaned her up and propped her on her side. Next morning, she found Tiffany in the same position, motionless, her skin dusky. Marla believes she had a heart attack during another seizure, but she'll never know. She could not admit her relief to anyone, not even her husband. "You'll change my name, right?" she asked repeatedly during our interview. She explains, "There is this sort of myth that parents with kids who are developmentally disabled are somehow altruistic, wonderful parents, and somehow God has given them all these extra tools. I've got this Erma Bombeck column that I cut out years ago about when God made mothers, he gave mothers of handicapped children this extra special something. Well, no. You do what you have to do." In fact, she and her husband had discussed, long ago, the possibility of giving up the care of their daughter when her needs became too great. "I remember when we first recognized how disabled Tiffany was. I thought, if there's ever a point where the burden of caring for her outweighs the satisfaction we get from caring for her, then that's the time to place her in a home. Because I had seen parents who had cared for children with severe disabilities at the expense of their own lives. I didn't want to be that way."

Still, she is aware of the pedestal people put her on and consequently finds herself caught in a paradox. "How can I say that I'm relieved that the burden of caring for my child is gone," she asks, "when it isn't supposed to be a burden?"

Heather Harris lost her baby son Joshua to a genetic defect called Trisomy 18. These babies, who have an extra number 18 chromosome, are born with a constellation of problems that include undersized brains and jaws, webbed fingers and toes, and heart, lung, and kidney defects. Although she knew that few live more than a year, and that most die shortly after birth, Heather, a delivery-room nurse, thought about the consequences of raising Joshua. "Trisomy 18 means severe mental retardation. He would never walk, talk, or eat on his own," she says. Joshua lived for four hours, and afterward Heather's emotions veered between grief and relief, with relief predominating. "My biggest feeling was, we were really spared," she says. "Our daily lives would have been very changed, for me especially. I'd be caring for him on a twenty-four-hour basis . . . my daughter would not be getting the attention she gets from us . . . it would have been a financial burden. I had seen families struggle." She has a memento of Joshua's short life that she treasures. "This may sound kind of funny, but it's a picture of me holding him after he died. His eyes are closed, and mine are closed, and it's the end of a long journey, that's the feeling. It sums up our journey together, and it's very peaceful."

Joan Nye's voice is full of pain as she tries to sort out the confusing facts of her son John's short life. When he was fourteen, the musically talented, studious, polite boy she knew suddenly turned into an unpredictable, sullen stranger. He began drinking, smoking, and doing drugs. He skipped school, shoplifted, and once Joan overheard him talking about whether to join some other boys in burglarizing houses. Sometimes at night, when she checked his bed, he was gone. Joan was baffled, and frantic. "From '94 on, he was never the same kid," she says. All three of John's parents—his dad, as well as Joan and her husband, Jerry, John's stepfather—tried everything to convince him to stay in high school—to no avail. Looking back, she knows now that John was seriously mentally ill, although for a long time she thought she was dealing with teenage rebellion and drugs. Only after he had periods when he seemed out of touch with reality, and attempted suicide, did she suspect that John was mentally ill. A psychiatrist prescribed medication for what he believed was bipolar disorder, but John self-medicated with street drugs instead. "He was good at masking and denying," she says. When John was fifteen, Joan had a realization that left her shaken. She and John had driven to Idaho for a wedding, and on the way they visited the graves of Joan's grandparents in Kalispell, Montana. "There was a third plot," she recalls, "that the family had forgotten was there, and I thought John might be there someday. I feared this boy was on a collision course with disaster."

Looking back, Joan says that during John's teenage years "I grieved for the child I'd lost, but the bigger emotion was worry, because I loved him so much. I was running from pillar to post, trying to find help." Both attorneys, Joan and Jerry had more connections in the legal and medical fields, as well as more money, than most parents. One night, when John came home stoned, Joan asked him if it was time to get help. "Yes," he admitted quietly. "My life is out of control." By then, one of Joan's friends had told her about "emotional growth" schools, designed for troubled adolescents. Maybe, she hoped, one of those would help John find his way. They enrolled him in one such school on the East Coast and, after that, a wilderness program in Oregon, and then, for his junior and senior years, a Quaker school in California. The tight structure of these schools seemed to help, at least for a while, and Joan began to hope John would finish high school. But the spring of his senior year was the beginning of the end. Although he had gotten good scores on his SATs and been accepted at three colleges, John swallowed a bottle of Tylenol and lay down in a field to die. Thankfully, before too much time had passed, he thought better of it and called Joan, who ordered him to go and find an adult. After a brief hospitalization, however, and although he had only five weeks until graduation, he refused to return to school.

Telling his mother he needed to search for "a life for himself," John packed up and began an odyssey that took him to New Mexico, where he lived for a few weeks. Finally, to Joan's immense relief, he told her he was on his way home. "Stay safe," she told him, not knowing that these were the last words she would ever say to her son. She didn't know that his car had broken down or that he had bought a bus ticket to Nevada, instead of Montana. In Mesquite, Nevada, he shot himself while waiting for the bus out of town.

Joan was sitting at her office computer when a policeman walked in. "He said, 'Ma'am, this isn't going to be easy,' and I knew what he was going to say." While she lives with lots of guilt, she takes comfort in the fact that a bevy of mental health "experts" couldn't help John either. As for relief, she protests, "I'm sure you understand that when I talk about relief, it doesn't mean I don't wish he were alive. I'd give anything to have John alive." Still, she continues, "I recognize the very difficult things that are now missing from my life." First among these is the all-consuming worry about her troubled son: his bad feelings about himself, his difficulties interacting with others, the terror they both endured during his psychic breaks. "I don't know if I was afraid for my physical safety," she says, "but there were some episodes of shouting when I wasn't sure what was going to happen." She doesn't miss watching him deteriorate, she says, or having to put her plans with Jerry constantly on hold. They couldn't leave home with John's mental state and behavior so unpredictable. Now, she says, she has a sense of closure. "I wanted John to have a real life," she says. "It was a combination of wistfulness and worry, that he wouldn't have the experiences other kids had." While John was alive, attending weddings and graduations was especially painful for her. "Now I don't have to wonder whether John will experience or enjoy these things." Even though the knowledge brings great sadness, it also brings a measure of resolution.

Her voice hardens when she cites another source of relief. "I don't have to listen to people say, 'You can't help him, you can only help yourself'"—advice that seems to sum up in a single phrase the bitter frustration, as well as the futility, of trying to help her son. She is still trying to make sense of the welter of emotions she wades through every day. "Every time I talk about John's mental illness, I feel I'm betraying him," she admits. She agrees that suicide is a hard type of death to grieve. At the same time, she says, "it's analogous to cancer patients' families, knowing that the patient's pain is over. I recognize that living meant a great deal of suffering for John."

Baby boomers have been dubbed "the sandwich generation" because many end up caring for aging parents as well as growing children. Tana Knowlton's eighty-eight-year-old mother, Abby, had had Alzheimer's for eight years when she fell and broke her hip. Tana's dad, Ted, in the same facility with her mom, had MS and had been bedridden for almost nine years. After hip surgery, Abby developed a serious infection and for two weeks lay in a hospital bed, sick and suffering. "You think about somebody in the death and dying process, and you don't think about it lasting ten years," Tana says plaintively. Tana had married a man with two children of his own, so between their four children, her two debilitated parents, and her stressful job as a college administrator, she felt stretched to the limit. She had pondered for many years whether visiting a mother who didn't know her anymore served any useful purpose. Consequently, she felt "a huge sense of relief" when Abby died. "I got a phone call from some-one at work," she says, "who was devastated that my mother had died. And I had to say, wait a minute, this is nothing like the deaths you've experienced in your life, sudden deaths of your father and brother. This is nothing like those. I am OK with this, this will not rock my world."

Her father has been hospitalized nine times with in-fections. Of the death still facing her, she says, "Part of my thing with my dad is, I'm kind of numb with going to the hospital, and having the nurse get in my face and say, 'You know, your dad may not live.' By all rights, there is no reason why my father should have outlived my mother. I think I'll be relieved when he dies. Maybe I should call you then?" We tell Tana she probably won't need to call; she will have every reason to feel relieved.

Al Stumph found his professional beliefs put to the test when his wife, Bonnie, became the primary caregiver for her mother, Marie, who had metastasized breast can-cer. Told in August 1998 that she would only live till Christmas, Marie surprised everyone by living another eight months.

For Al, it was a lonely, frustrating time. At first Bonnie came home two or three nights a week, but as Marie de-clined she spent more and more time at her mother's house. Always close, several of Bonnie's seven sisters came and went, helping care for their mother. Although there would have been room in Marie's large house, Bon-nie didn't want Al to stay there. It was hard for him to ac-cept his banishment, but he tried to be understanding. "This was something Bonnie and her sisters had to experience together," he says. Coming home to an empty house was the worst time of day for Al, who desperately missed his wife's company. He fed their dog and two cats and puttered in his wood shop, then went to bed alone.

Al didn't resent Marie; he loved and missed her, too. They shared the same religion, Catholicism, as well as similar political beliefs and senses of humor. Of course he wanted the best for her, particularly at the end of her life. But even more constricting was the fact that Al, a social worker, changed jobs after Marie's illness, taking a job as director of an elder services agency. The agency's time-honored policy was that every effort be made toward keeping the elderly in their own homes.

Al believed that, too. *But what about me?* he sometimes wanted to ask, on the nights when silence echoed around him. "I never had any theoretical problems with elderly people staying in their homes," he says. "But I did feel boxed in. These ideas tend to be harder in practice than they are in theory." He found himself in the unenviable position of being abandoned, with no one to complain to.

The flood of relief he felt when Marie died and Bonnie finally returned made him feel guilty, even as he realized his relief was justified. "I felt guilty that it was because of Marie's death that I had Bonnie back," he says, but in the end his social work background helped him, just as it had hurt him for a while. "Relief and guilt are normal human emotions."

4

Relationship Relief

"Now I'm prayin' for the end of time, so I can end my time with you . . . "

—Meat Loaf

Jennifer's story:

When I look back at pictures of myself during my marriage to Paul, I am struck by how gaunt and tired I look. Every day was a contest to see if I could measure up to his directives about what my role would be, how I should look and act, who my friends should be. Because Paul ridiculed my friends, I let my friendships lapse rather than risk starting yet another argument with him. That meant I grew increasingly lonely and isolated, too.

I wasn't allowed to mow the lawn, because, according to Paul, a doctor's wife didn't do menial work. I couldn't wear blue jeans to the post office (too casual) or wear a dress that came above my knees (too provocative) even though it was 1983. Paul was always worried that I might do or say something to embarrass him in public, despite my college degree. "Don't say anything. You'll only sound stupid," he'd warn, or, "Now, let me do the talking here," when we encountered someone whose opinion counted to him, which, I sometimes reflected, was practically everyone except me. Back at home, the tension that smoldered in public ignited in private, and he sometimes picked up handy objects, like dishes, to throw at me.

One incident comes back to me vividly. Although I was in active labor with our daughter, Paul told me to take our two huge trash cans around to the back of the house, in case we had visitors after the baby was born. Although my contractions were intense, I did as I was told. There was no use arguing with Paul. I had learned long ago that the appearance of the house and yard were much more important to him than my comfort. Before we left for the hospital, newspapers had to be tidied up, dishes done, beds made, trash cans moved. Elizabeth was born five minutes after I got to the hospital.

She was the brightest spot in our marriage, and my memory of the day of her birth is still radiant with joy, despite the acrimony between Paul and me. For a brief moment, Paul and I were drawn into the circle of wonder and enchantment that surrounded our newborn daughter. Again I allowed myself to hope that all would be well, that there would be a happily-ever-after for us after all.

That illusion disappeared when Paul came to bring us home from the hospital. I had spent many months happily anticipating the arrival of my baby. My cousin Jan, who had introduced Paul and me, had loaned me boxes of wonderfully soft hand-me-down baby clothes, and I had picked out an adorable outfit printed with Snoopys for the trip home. It was warm and soft—just what I wanted against my precious daughter's skin. But Paul had different ideas. A gift had arrived from a couple who lived in our town, and the husband was a state legislator, one of our more prominent citizens. The gift was a stiff pink taffeta dress with matching plastic pants and scratchy lace around the collar, cuffs, and legs. Over my protests and tears, Paul insisted that I dress Elizabeth in it. "There's a group of people waiting at home," he told me, "and this will make a big hit."

I saw then and there that Elizabeth, like me, was destined to be a reflection of his perfect world rather than a person in her own right. At home I sat upstairs, tears falling on Elizabeth's blanket as I rocked her, listening to my husband and his mother argue downstairs in the kitchen. I wanted my child to grow up strong and independent, to learn how to make her own decisions, but I had little hope of Paul allowing that. After he died, I realized that Elizabeth would now have a chance to grow into the person she was meant to be. And so would I . . .

When someone dies who has been a constant source of criticism, abuse, oppression, or anxiety, "relationship relief" is the result.

For Gloria Reed, her husband Nick's death was the answer to a prayer, which for Gloria has a certain irony, since she met Nick through her church. Looking back, she wonders if he wasn't using the church to hide—from his abusiveness, alcoholism, and homosexuality. But that's been since his death. Back then, she thought he was wonderful.

Gloria didn't have the happiest history either. Her first husband had left her for another woman when she was seven months pregnant with her second son. But dreams die hard, and she still hoped to find a good man who would be a loving father to her two boys, Todd, fourteen, and T.J., twelve. Although at first she didn't care for Nick—he was a bit of a know-it-all, she thought—other church members seemed to like him, and she kept encountering him at church functions. Eventually she accepted a date with him. He drove her to a steak house in a neighboring town, and they danced till the wee hours. She had to admit he was a good dancer and a good conversationalist, even if he seemed to overdo the cocktails a bit. At premarital counseling sessions, Nick was careful to give their minister the right answers. And to her delight, he was good with the boys. He played in an adult softball league, coached Little League, and spent hours working with Todd and T.J. on their batting techniques or just playing catch. Gloria, single for so long, found herself falling in love. She and Nick were married on Valentine's Day 1998.

Almost immediately Nick's personality began to show cracks, like a house on a bad foundation. When he drank, which was every night, he belittled and teased the boys, especially Todd, who was less athletic than his younger brother. Hoping to rekindle some of the earlier magic, Gloria made reservations at the steak house where their romance had begun. But on the way there, Nick stayed glued to his portable phone, making one business call after another. When he asked Gloria to hold the phone for a moment, she impulsively rolled down the car window and mimed throwing it out. Nick, enraged, grabbed her arm and screamed himself hoarse. They ate in tense silence. At home he threw her down on the bed and tried to choke her. "Why do you always make me do these things?" he croaked.

Gloria began to fear for herself and her marriage, but she prayed Nick would change. She dreaded a second divorce, remembering the feelings of self-blame and depression that had followed the first. When Nick began to pick on Todd one evening, Gloria picked a fight with Nick, a maneuver that sometimes deflected his wrath from her sons. This time he held her down on the bed, slapped her, and screamed in her face till Todd called 911. Gloria managed to get away and lock herself in the bathroom, which is where the police found her. She and the boys went to a safehouse. Although Nick was contrite, apologizing and sending flowers, this time Gloria, frightened, stayed put. A few nights later she tried to call him at their home but got no answer. She thought he was trying to give her a dose of her own medicine, and she waited till next evening to call again. "He could be so vindictive, so mean," she says. When again there was no answer, she went to the house. Seeing the newspapers outside and hearing the dogs barking inside, she felt a shiver of foreboding. Nick was face down on their bed, and his leg, when she gingerly touched it, felt cold and hard as a rock. Hysterical, Gloria called 911. "My husband is dead!" she screamed, over and over, unable to get beyond that single, horrifying fact.

In the following days, the community poured itself into memorial services and tributes to Nick, who had been widely admired as a businessman who supported a variety of community causes, and generously gave his time to coach Little League. Gloria sat through the services with her own memories. When she and her minister went to Nick's office to clean out his desk, they discovered computer files full of gay pornography, as well as catalogs of gay sex toys. Of all the offenses Gloria had endured, this one hurt the worst. Now she understood why Nick had so rarely initiated sex and why he found excuses to spend time at his office alone. "When I found out about the pornography," she says, "I wanted to go out to the cemetery, dig him up, and kill him all over again."

Although she was furious with Nick, she was riddled with guilt. Nick had had epilepsy but was not always careful about taking his pills. He must have had a seizure and suffocated, face-down in the bed clothes. Gloria felt terrible that she had not been there to save him. For months before he died she had prayed that God would keep her and the boys safe. But she hadn't meant for Nick to die.

At the services she felt as if she were mourning a different Nick from the rest of the world. She heard her abusive husband described as "intense," a man who "told it like it was," but that was as close as anyone got to her reality. His brother and parents knew about the abuse but never referred to it. Nick's aunt advised her to "just forget about all the bad things about Nick and grieve for the loss of the good."

There weren't many good memories. Her marriage had been brief, only sixteen months, but for Gloria it had felt endless. Whoever it was—God or fate or dumb luck—something had intervened in getting her out of a monstrous choice of a marriage partner. Gloria was more than ready to put the past behind her. She sold the living-room furniture that had belonged to Nick and put up pictures of her family, something Nick had forbidden her to do. She is determined that if she remarries it will be to someone very different from Nick.

When a spouse with a controlling personality contracts a chronic illness, a bad situation gets even worse. Lenore Lansing was married to her husband Ed for forty-two years, and for the last ten of them Ed had a lung disease known as chronic obstructive pulmonary disease (COPD), which made it hard for him to breathe. "Anyone who has a lung dysfunction becomes kind of angry," Lenore says. "He was angry a lot, sudden outbursts over little things. I think all of us had to learn to just kind of put up with it because Dad was sick."

Their marriage had hardly been idyllic before the illness, but at least Ed looked at parenthood as a joint effort and helped Lenore raise their two children, John and Sheila. The Lansings lived in a small town, with Ed the only lawyer for miles around. An avid hunter, he owned an extensive gun collection, and Lenore sometimes felt she was being watched by the many trophy heads of mountain sheep, deer, elk, moose, and antelope that covered the walls of their home.

Sometimes she wanted to scream at the claustrophobia of living with her tyrannical husband in their tiny fishbowl of a community. Ed kept tabs on her every move and felt threatened by any success—no matter how small—that Lenore enjoyed. For a time she worked as a guidance counselor in the local high school, but when she ended up representing the victim in a court case he was involved in, he made her quit. Restless at home, she went into private practice counseling, but Ed complained when clients called her at home, so she gave that up, too. Even when she wasn't working, he accused her of entertaining men while he was at work. She threatened to leave him unless they got marriage counseling, but, at Ed's insistence, they had to drive nearly 100 miles to another town to keep it a secret. Raised Catholic, Lenore couldn't bring herself to leave him.

In the last months of his life, Ed's increasing shortness of breath was matched by a shortness of temper. "He would yell, scream, throw things, put his fist through the door," she says. "I thought, 'It's better than if he hit me.'" The days were long for Lenore, who feared the drawn-out gasping for breath that Ed's death from COPD would surely bring. But like Dick Appling's wife Marijane, who died quickly of lung cancer, Ed's death, mercifully, came from a deadly disease: colon cancer that had gone undetected because of his lung problems. He was dead within a month of diagnosis.

Besides the relief of Ed's fairly painless death (he had a morphine pump), Lenore was relieved to be out of her marriage at last. Her children knew what their father had been like, and she was able to talk freely to John and Sheila. She also had two sets of couple friends who knew Ed's domineering side. Otherwise, she had no one else to confide in. "Over the years, I did lots of pretending, and doing things on my own," she says. People in her tiny town had nothing but admiration for her husband. "Ed did a lot of estate planning and probate work," she says. "I tell you, those little old ladies thought he was such a wonderful person, who did such a good job. I didn't want to go on the rest of my life hearing that, I really didn't."

Although she couldn't summon up much sadness for Ed, Lenore grieved for the marriage she'd never had. She remembered as a young girl picturing married life as blissful, which had not been at all true for her. She wondered if she had done the right thing, staying with Ed for so many years. Now she was sixty-three, young for widowhood, maybe, but old for the dating scene. She began attending a hospice support group, hoping to make some sense of her feelings. At one session, Lenore was the only one who showed up, and she found herself opening up about the disappointment her marriage had been—and the positive things about Ed's death. The young therapist who ran the group told Lenore about her own mother's relief when her dad died, both because he had mistreated her mother, and because his death from lupus had been long and painful. Lenore was grateful. "I don't know if it was right for her to share confidences," Lenore muses. "But in the end, it helped me."

Within a few months, Lenore held a big garage sale, and people gleefully paid bottom dollar for Ed's guns and expensive clothes—and the despised trophy heads. She sold the house and moved to another town where fewer people knew Ed. It's been lonelier for her, and she battles a weight problem because of the loneliness, but at least she doesn't have to keep up a charade anymore. "I feel relief that I don't have to worry about trying to keep the marriage going, to keep him happy, to keep sanity within the home. Every day is calm. I was reading something the other day, and the word 'unanxiety' was used. I'm not sure if it's a word, but I thought yes, that's it. There's no more anxiety. I no longer have to live a lie."

Lenore is fortunate in being able to share her relief with her children and a few friends. She was also lucky to find a grief therapist who not only affirmed her but also was able to reinforce that affirmation by sharing an experience of her own. Not everyone who goes in search of help will find someone so empathic. Some therapists may find your nontraditional affect symptomatic of some deeper pathology or expect you to fit into some preconceived mold. This may do you harm. Because grief can make us feel so out of control, and none of us has an individual road map of how to get through it, a griever may begin to question her own response to a loss, especially if she finds herself criticized. If she takes up the five stages as her guide, she may find herself completely off the map. If, convinced that her feelings are indeed abnormal, she enlists the aid of a therapist who also sees them as problematic, she may be setting herself up for further self-doubt, confusion, and guilt. No wonder many grievers find themselves "slapped by the helping hand."

The field of grief therapy has been dominated by a few well-known researchers who have seen nontraditional grievers as not quite right. Rather than ask whether the griever might have good reasons for feeling relieved, grief studies have tended to come from the viewpoint that there is a "right way" to grieve, because it's the way most people grieve. This point of view has disenfranchised many perfectly healthy people.

Modern theories of psychology owe a great debt to British psychologist John Bowlby, who in the 1960s developed the concept of attachment, which underpins much bereavement theory today. Bowlby believed that a baby, by being cuddled and comforted, formed an attachment to her parents, because they were the source of security. As the child grew, this attachment became emotional as well, and love developed between parent and child. The crying and searching behavior Bowlby observed when he separated babies from their mothers, he believed, were grief reactions.

Because protesting the disruption of the attachment bond followed naturally if the attachment had been secure, Bowlby felt that not feeling sad after a death was unnatural. He described two types of euphoria following a death, and he believed both were aberrant. Type One is characterized by the mourner's inability or refusal to believe that the deceased has died, and the giddy feeling comes from the belief that the deceased is actually still alive. In Type Two, the bereaved person has acknowledged the loss and feels a sense of betterment. Both of these, he felt, stemmed from an inability to form an attachment to the person who had died.

With human beings as complex as they are, however, maybe it's possible to form an attachment to someone and still be relieved at his death. It's altogether possible to truly love some aspects of a person and detest others. This is particularly true in the case of addictions. "I loved my husband when he wasn't drinking," said one widow, "and hated him when he was." People also grieve for what might have been, as Lenore Lansing found herself doing when she grieved the happy marriage she'd never had.

Psychologist Colin Murray Parkes found that certain bereaved people, following an unhappy marriage, experienced an initial sense of relief, but this was followed by self-doubt, guilt, remorse, and a continued need to feel close to the deceased. Following Bowlby's thinking, he speculated that someone involved in an unhappy marriage must have lower self-esteem and thus was likely to have problems recovering a healthy identity after the spouse died. In a study of London widows, Parkes provides an example of a widow whose lack of grieving strikes him as unhealthy. "Mrs. F" is described as having had a "somewhat distant relationship" with her husband, "but they had never quarreled." After his death, Parkes relates, Mrs. F "felt very shocked, but experienced no other emotion for three weeks." As time went on, Mrs. F "expressed little need to grieve for her husband." Yet he criticizes Mrs. F's lack of grief: "The fact that she had not had a close love relationship with her husband *enabled her to pretend* that she had nothing to grieve for, and that life could go on in much the same way as it had before his death."

Looking at the multitude of studies, we would seem to know a lot about grief, but this impression would be misleading. For every study that purports to prove one thing, another claims to prove the opposite. In an intriguing article ("The Myths of Coping with Loss," 1989), sociologists Camille Wortman and Roxane Silver questioned some common assumptions, the most prevalent being that bereaved people should be intensely distressed about a death—otherwise there will be hell to pay eventually. As one popular book advised, "Silence or 'stiff upper lip' approach to grief causes inner turmoil and eventual problems. Grief feelings linger and emerge in some other way later on."

However, Wortman and Silver found that such a reaction was by no means universal—and that those who did not seem particularly distressed did no worse in the long run (although in the studies, the "long run" was only two years) than those who were very upset. In fact, they point out that exactly the opposite was true: Those who were most depressed immediately after the death were likely to still be depressed two years later.

Wortman and Silver also questioned Bowlby's assertion that someone who is not particularly distressed is psychologically incapable of forming attachments and found nothing to support this assumption. Parents who had lost babies to SIDS, for example, yet who did not seem to be particularly grief-stricken, were just as likely to describe their babies as "beautiful," "intelligent," and "happy" as were parents who were very upset; in other words, their attachment to their dead infants was as strong as the very distressed group.

Many grief therapists caution the bereaved against entering into new relationships before they have completed their "grief work." Believing the old adage that "women grieve, men replace," they warn widowers in particular against jumping into romance too soon. Yet the authors know of a number of widows and widowers who remarried within a year of their spouses' deaths whose marriages seem very happy. Apparently, for some, replacing a spouse does work!

What can we conclude from this? Maybe the only thing we can say with certainty is that people are unique in their coping mechanisms, relationships, and circumstances and that "unhealthy" ways of coping must be determined on an individual basis.

Ken Nichols certainly wouldn't define himself as unhealthy, even though he feels relieved not just that his wife is dead but that she chose such a gracious way out.

By the time Eileen died, Ken had long forgotten the good years. He had met her on a blind date, and they married a few years later. She was his rock during medical school and residency to become a pediatrician. His voice is wistful as he talks about that time. "There's a song called 'The Hungry Years,'" he says, "and it talks about ketchup sandwiches, and spending your quarter a week on the movies because that's all the money you have, and walking everyplace, and eating spaghetti seven days a week. That's what we did when I was in medical school, and it was great." He deeply loved his wife, a former debutante who came from money yet left all that behind to live with him in a cramped third-floor apartment, help support him financially, and bear his children, a daughter while he was still in medical school and, eventually, two sons.

But the good years didn't last long. After the birth of their third child, Eileen slid into a postpartum depression that never lifted. Each new psychiatrist had a different diagnosis—paranoid schizophrenia, affective disorder, bipolar disease. The only constant was that Eileen got sicker. While the kids were growing up, she was in and out of mental hospitals, sometimes for months at a time. Often, she called him at his busy pediatric practice, threatening to kill herself if he didn't come home immediately. "Well, I had an office full of patients, and I'd leave them and get home," he remembers. "More than once, she was lying on the floor full of pills, or she had cut her wrists, and I would have to take her up to the hospital."

Formerly attractive and well-groomed, she grew obese and stopped bathing. She also became violent with Ken, slapping and kicking—and worse. "Sometimes she threatened me with a knife," he says. "I don't believe in hitting people, so I took a course in karate. Ostensibly, it was to protect my medical bag in parking lots, but it was really to protect me from my wife." Because she sometimes wandered around during the night, he resorted to tying his leg to hers so that any movement would wake him up.

During her manic phases, Eileen could be surprisingly organized and determined, and she managed to earn a master's degree in social work a few years before she died. Because she seemed to be in one of those modes when she told him she planned to go on a tour of Bali, Ken had no inkling that she was going to kill herself there. Maybe she didn't know. When Ken answered the phone late one afternoon, it was the tour director, telling him that Eileen was ill and had been taken by ambulance to the nearest large city. After a few hours of agonized waiting, the hospital called to say that Eileen was, in fact, dead.

Ken's first thought was, after seventeen years of threats, *What a classy thing to do.* "She had these caches of pills all over the place, so I don't know what she took," he says. "The autopsy is in Indonesian, and I could find someone to translate it for me, but I don't need to read it. All I need to know is that she is dead." She had left no note. He didn't even have to fly to Bali; his local funeral home made arrangements with the state department to ship her body home.

"If I had to choose one word to describe how life is different," he says slowly, "that word would be 'free.' I love her for the children, I love her for the first five years of our marriage, I love her for killing herself where I don't have to feel guilty because I couldn't help her. My attitude is, Eileen is at peace, and by God, so am I."

Like Lenore Lansing's use of the word "unanxiety," Ken's choice of the word "free" is one many other relieved grievers could use to describe themselves. Maybe they would also identify with the German word *Schadenfreude*, which translates as "happy-sad." It's unfortunate that English has no equivalent, because we English-speakers certainly have the emotion. *Schadenfreude* perfectly describes the feeling of lightness and peace that can coexist with the heaviness of regret or sadness. *Schadenfreude* also implies a sense of spite, which may be harder to admit, but grievers who have managed to outlive someone who has been a source of pain can be forgiven if they feel a tad triumphant. They are alive, whereas their persecutor is dead.

A group of relieved grievers not to be overlooked are the "blooming widows," a phenomenon often observed by hospice workers. Particularly among the generation that married during or just after World War II, marriage was expected to last until death. Although more unhappy wives tended to stay in bad marriages because the husband earned the paycheck, men of that generation also tended to think of marriage as a lifelong commitment. In this age group, the widow or widower who finds herself or himself without a partner for the first time in many years may also find the freedom to pursue new interests and hobbies in a way that wasn't possible before. An animal lover married to an allergic spouse can now have cats; a wife who has always wanted to travel but was paired with a stay-at-home husband can now indulge her wanderlust.

Demographically, wives are much more likely to outlive, and therefore end up caring for, their husbands. We can't help but wonder if evolution designed women, socialized to be the more nurturing sex, to live longer so that they would be around to care for their ailing husbands. Widows who married in an earlier era may find themselves, following their husband's deaths, reborn into a world that didn't exist then, a place where women have a wider variety of roles and encounter fewer restrictions to pursue their own goals. If they find themselves well-off financially, they may find a new world opening up for them. In *The Corrections*, Jonathan Franzen's National Book Award–winning saga of a Midwestern family, matriarch Enid Lambert finds herself in just this position:

> [Alfred] had been living at the Deepmire Home
> for two years when he stopped accepting food.

Chip took time away from parenthood and his new teaching job at a private high school and his eighth revision of the screenplay to visit from Chicago and say good-bye. Alfred lasted longer after that than anyone expected. He was a lion to the end. His blood pressure was barely measurable when Denise and Gary flew into town, and still he lived another week. He lay curled up on the bed and barely breathed. He moved for nothing and responded to nothing except to shake his head emphatically, once, if Enid tried to put an ice chip in his mouth. The one thing he never forgot was how to refuse. All of her correction had been for naught. He was as stubborn as the day she'd met him. And yet when he was dead, when she'd pressed her lips to his forehead and walked out with Denise and Gary into the warm spring night, she felt that nothing could kill her hope now, nothing. She was seventy-five and she was going to make some changes in her life.

The marriage need not have been unhappy for a widow to exult in her new life. Celia Schroeder's husband of fifty years left her with a trust fund, a lovely home, and plenty of fond memories. Although she loved him deeply, she finds much to like about widowhood as well. Of the changes that have followed Ed's death, she says, "I don't mind living alone. I've never lived by myself before, and I kind of like it. I have lots of friends. I go out to lunch and to dinner and to church. I am fortunate enough financially that I can have my lawn done and a cleaning crew come in once a month. I never lack for something to do. All of my friends are widows and we often go out to eat together."

Widowers can also bloom. Author Catherine Sanders, developer of the "Grief Experience Inventory," writes of a seventy-five-year-old widower who experienced, as she terms it, a *liberating* death. After the couple moved to Florida to enjoy a leisurely retirement, the man's wife refused to let him participate in any of the activities he had looked forward to. She acquired one psychosomatic illness after another in order to keep him by her side. When she died during elective surgery, he was surprised and relieved to find himself free to pursue his hobbies. He had no need of grief therapy, and within two years he had begun to date. Sanders calls his situation a "God-given divorce" and notes that professional intervention, given this man's healthy adjustment, would only have hindered his progress.

Marriage partners are a choice, and miserable though the process usually is, it is always possible to divorce an unbearable husband or wife. However, a quarrelsome blood relative is another matter entirely, because no court proceeding can dissolve a blood tie. It's likely that the sense of relief at such a death is even more profound than the death of a spouse, as in Karen Cox's case. "Overall, there was a sense of relief that never left, and is with me to this day," Karen says of her mother Josefina's death.

Josefina rebuffed all Karen's attempts, both as a child and as an adult, to establish a loving relationship. Even though her mother had died twelve years before our interview, in that time Karen hadn't talked to anyone besides her husband concerning her feelings after Josefina's death. She described a feeling of "lightness," as if a huge weight had been lifted. "Parts of her were strong, but parts were very damaged," she says.

The daughter of Lithuanian immigrants, Josefina had had a brutal childhood herself. Both her parents had been alcoholic, and the family lived in grinding poverty. Karen caught hints that sexual abuse went on, too, although Josefina never elaborated. Karen felt pity for her mother, which helped ease her disappointment about Josefina's lack of warmth. Particularly wounding was the fact that Josefina was vivacious and talkative with her friends, a side of her personality she never showed Karen. *What's wrong with me?* Karen agonized. *Why can't she show me just a little of what she shows her friends?* When Josefina, whose own alcoholism added another painful layer to an already bad relationship, lay dying of breast cancer, she refused even to squeeze Karen's hand as she kept a deathbed vigil. For Karen, who loved her mother in spite of her neglect, knowing that Josefina remained alert and aware, and was in pain to the end, was very difficult. But realizing that now she, Karen, could lay her own burden down was also liberating.

Joy Stevens grew up feeling loved but out of place, like a bluebird in a nest of sparrows. Bright, adventuresome, and athletic, she always felt like an oddity in her conservative Christian parents' lives. Raised during the Depression, with only eighth-grade educations, her parents valued marriage, family, and fitting in; they couldn't understand Joy's aspirations toward higher education and world travel. After high school, she moved from her small Southern town to a big city, where she got an LPN license as well as a degree in psychology. She took up archery, skiing, and hunting, attended some Quaker meetings, and even explored Buddhism, which would have horrified her parents, had she told them. "It wasn't that I wasn't good enough, just that I never fit their ideal," she says. As an adult, when she would call from Russia, Australia, or Jamaica, her dad couldn't keep the disapproval out of his voice. "The world is never big enough for Joy," he'd say. Both her elderly parents have died in the last three years. Today, she says, "I realize I can be on this planet without someone significant to me disapproving of me. The little dark shadow or cloud that was there is gone."

A problem in-law can be almost as troublesome as a blood relative, because being married to your spouse means having to interact with your in-laws also. Beth Durkee and her mother-in-law, Ann, were near the same age when Beth married Ann's stepson, Allen. Beth's two sons by a previous marriage were close in age to Ann's daughter and son, and at first the two women were friends, taking the kids on outings and picnics together. Beth had always dreamed of having her own business designing jewelry, so when she decided to attend a gemology school in another state, Allen supported her decision and agreed to care for the boys for nine months. When Beth returned home, however, her reception from Ann was icy. Although she wouldn't speak to Beth directly, according to Allen, Ann was disgusted that Beth would leave her sons to selfishly indulge her "hobby." Beth was devastated. "I truly believe that she never forgave me," she says. "I never felt warmth from her again." She thinks now that Ann, who had never attended college, was jealous, and Beth blames herself for not trying to reach out to her. But at the time, Ann's coldness was too forbidding. For five years, the women struggled to maintain a polite facade. Beth's father-in-law took his wife's side and also began to snub Beth. Then Ann discovered a mass in her stomach, and by the time she went for an ultrasound, her tumor was so advanced that surgery couldn't remove it all. "It was eight months of dying slowly," says Beth. When she could, she avoided visiting Ann's hospital room; the feeling she got from Ann was "that little witch Beth is just a troublemaker."

Beth is still tormented by her feelings surrounding Ann's death. She feels guilty for not feeling sad when Ann died, and she wishes she had tried harder to reconcile with her mother-in-law. "But then I think, 'Dammit, she didn't try either,'" Beth says. Ann's death at age forty-seven had been long and miserable, with constant vomiting and increasingly powerful narcotics to ease the pain. Surprisingly, and distressingly, says Beth, "Even with Ann gone, the resentment has not gone away. The junk is still there. It's crappy."

Indeed, even with a liberating loss, guilt and unfinished business can be formidable obstacles to moving on with one's life. But even though the person is no longer around, there are ways to make peace.

5

Guilt

"*There is nothing either good or bad, but thinking
makes it so.*"

—Shakespeare
Hamlet

So prevalent and insidious is the feeling of guilt after
someone dies that some psychologists have argued
that it's a necessary part of the recovery process—so necessary, in fact, that if we don't have anything to feel guilty
about, we'll create something. In fact, one woman confessed to "feeling guilty for not feeling guilty." Yes, guilt is
the gift that keeps on giving.

According to a hospice worker who has been in the
field for a dozen years, "The experience of relief comes
with lots of guilt. People feel guilty because they get tired
of caregiving and wish the person would die, then after
the death, they feel guilty because they had that wish. As
hospice workers, the best thing we can give people is to
tell them it's normal to have those wishes. They're only

human." Chris recently received a letter praising her 1999 book, *Surviving Your Spouse's Chronic Illness*. The letter-writer, in her forties, wrote that her husband had been di-agnosed with MS a few years earlier and was now in a nursing home because of cognitive problems. "While my mother is saying novenas for a slow progression," she wrote candidly, "I'm hoping this will all end as quickly as possible, for my husband's sake as well as my own."

Precisely because of sentiments like this, Therese Rando asserts that long, chronic illnesses often leave a lin-gering residue of guilt in their wake. Survivors may even feel, on some primitive level, that their wishes somehow led to the death. Sigmund Freud was the first to write that, because all of us wish each other dead at times, even in the best relationships, seeing those wishes fulfilled could lead to complicated grief. Inside each of us lives the child who believes he is all-powerful.

When caregiving becomes necessary, the feelings of resentment that threaten to taint a previously happy rela-tionship can take us by surprise. Women, in particular, may feel obligated to care for a sick parent or husband, then find themselves resenting the obligation, then feeling guilty at the resentment. Stephanie Kellogg's beloved mother had a serious stroke and required more and more care, which Stephanie dedicated herself to providing per-sonally. "I did feel guilty when she was still alive that I was becoming resentful for having to provide that care for her, and having it be such a big part of my life," she says. "I felt guilty because, after all, she was my mother. She took care of me when I was growing up, and the least I could do was take care of her now."

Sean Grady had every reason to wish that his eighty-eight-year-old mother, Moira, would die. Sean's marriage to an alcohol- and drug-addicted woman was in deep trouble, and the niece he hired to take care of his mother was beginning to complain that she thought Moira would die within six months, and here it was eight. Sean's stressful job at a research facility meant he worked at least sixty hours per week. He loved his mother, who had raised him and his three siblings with little help from an alcoholic husband. He found himself thinking, "My God, when this is over, life will be so simple." Then he'd be overcome with guilt. "I didn't want to hurry her along," he insists. "I wanted her to take her time." He saw his resentment of her dying as selfish, especially since his study of Eastern religions taught that this could be a rich time for Moira, a sacred time. "And here I was, trying to rob her of this experience simply out of a sense of convenience."

When an illness has gone on for years, it's natural to wish for the end, as Chris knows.

Chris's story:

Being raised Catholic, I do guilt very well. During Don's illness I felt guilty that I was healthy, that my body still functioned as it was supposed to. I think this was a kind of "survivor guilt," but it made me feel as if I had to do everything possible to make my husband's life easier, because I was the healthy one. That made it difficult to determine what exactly I should do for him, and what I should let others do, or leave undone. Too, I was always questioning whether I "deserved" to do something fun, because he was so helpless. Eventually, I learned to forgive myself for my healthy body, and to tell myself I needed to take the horseback riding lessons I enjoyed so much, or to get away for a weekend for a vacation, otherwise there would be nothing for me to give Don or my two young children. I eventually realized these took nothing away from him, and did a lot for me.

I'll always wish I had been there for more of his dying. But I remind myself, that I'm saying this from a standpoint of now, feeling rested and fulfilled. At the time, I was exhausted and angry and depleted—as anyone would have been after fifteen years of this dreadful illness.

Then, I felt as if I were constantly trapped in a cycle of turbulent emotions, wishing the ordeal were over and then feeling guilty for those wishes, then angry at myself for feeling guilty. And so on . . . and on. If anything good has come from this experience, it has been in making me more compassionate of other well spouses and their choices.

It's logical, after a death, to take stock of our own role in the process. *Did I do enough to help?* Some have no problem at all answering the question. "What could I have done that I didn't do?" one woman asked rhetorically after her mother's long dying. "Nothing. Not a single thing."

Others have more trouble. Dick Appling, whose wife Marijane had Alzheimer's, says that the sheer physical relief he has felt since she died has been "immense." When the Alzheimer's began to make Marijane take off in fits of rage across the fields around his house, "It would flash into my mind, 'Maybe something will happen to her.' I didn't want it to, but it flashed into my mind." Dick, a former mining engineer, says that nowadays when guilt arises he calls on his powers of logic to keep it in check. While Marijane was alive, he researched chelation therapy, a method of removing heavy metals from the blood, and found a doctor who agreed to administer it, a therapy Dick believes bought her precious time. "I do feel guilty sometimes, but I get it under control. In the first place, I know I did everything I could. I did more than anyone could. I am absolutely convinced that I gave her at least two or three reasonably good years because of all this research I did. So I have no guilt feelings in that respect. But I think I have guilt from my feelings of relief." At those times, getting busy is his antidote—helping his ill sister, or his daughter with her family, or assisting at the nursing home where Marijane spent her last months.

Celia Schroeder's husband Ed had Alzheimer's also, but her "guilt remedy" is different from Dick's. Ed was so fit that at age eighty-one he was still riding his bike twenty-five miles a day, but Celia, afraid that he might get lost or have an accident, insisted that someone accompany him. When she caught him sneaking the bike out of the garage, she had her daughter pick it up and take it to her house. Ed was in a nursing home for only five months before he died, for which Celia is truly grateful. By then, she wanted him to die. "To see Ed like that and then to think that he would never be like he was . . ." she can't finish the thought. Nonetheless, after his death, she felt guilty over feeling relief. She reached out for reassurance. "My minister and friends assured me I had done everything I could have," she says. Her friends confirmed her own sense of her actions, and her guilt left quickly. She thinks now that it was a necessary part of her grieving. She also attended an Alzheimer's support group when Ed was alive, and some in the group have become her close friends. They remind her how hard it was. "We always talk about Alzheimer's and our husbands, and I think that is good," she says thoughtfully.

Getting rid of guilt can take years. For Shelly Pearson, it's taken almost two decades for the guilt of her first husband's death to dissipate. She met Mel as a freshman in college and was immediately attracted to his dark good looks and brilliant mind. The fact that his intelligence was accompanied by a mercurial temperament added to his allure. Sprung for the first time from a repressive fundamentalist Christian family, Shelly was reveling in her newfound freedom, and she and Mel were drawn into the collegiate fast lane. They moved in together.

When Mel's parents found out about their living arrangement, they issued an ultimatum: Get married, or Mel would be cut out of the family. So, although Shelly was only nineteen, they married. She knew Mel had scars; when he was fifteen, a neighbor girl several years older had developed a crush on him. When he ignored her advances, she furiously accused him of rape. His parents believed her, and their betrayal had been a devastating rejection for him. He was also one-quarter Navajo, and the family considered its Native American ancestry an embarrassment best concealed.

Mel discovered a gift for working with developmentally disabled kids and, after college, interviewed for a teaching job. When the grant funding fell through at the last minute, he was crushed. He took a job managing a local fast-food restaurant. Having to work at a job he hated added to his tendency toward depression, which in turn worsened when he self-medicated with alcohol and drugs. As the lows got steadily lower, he looked to Shelly to pull him out of himself. She tried. "I figured if we were good enough and strong enough, we could overcome anything," she says. "I had young, idealistic expectations."

But constantly trying to shore up her needy husband, to be the buffer between him and the world, drained her. Feeling trapped and oppressed, she told Mel she was moving out and ending their four-year marriage. He began to threaten suicide, telling her he would take his Harley and run it into a bridge. Naively, Shelly dismissed it as just talk—until the day the phone rang at work and a voice asked if she was Mel's wife. The police thought he might have hit a patch of ice, but Shelly knew the truth.

In the skies on the way to his funeral, Shelly began a dialogue in her head with her troubled young husband. *Why didn't I do something to stop this? Why did I abandon you? Why didn't I know this was real?* she sobbed. She even felt responsible for the fate of Mel's soul because he had died violently. There was no end to the blame she laid at her own door.

She was also mightily relieved. "I didn't have to deal anymore with his insanity or intensity. I only had me to feel responsible for. I watched other people go through divorces where the ex was there creating havoc, and that was something I didn't have to worry about. I was happy Mel was out of pain, because he was very unhappy and lost."

The guilt she felt, both for what she saw as her failure to save him and for her feelings of relief, remained with her long after she remarried and had two children. Continuing to talk to Mel in her head, as she had for the first time on the plane, helped lift the blackness she felt. She dreamed that he appeared to her and told her that he was in a better place and no longer in pain. He entrusted her with the secret of his suicide; his parents didn't know, and he would never want them to.

Shelly's study of Eastern religions has helped her resolve her feelings of responsibility. She and Mel had both believed in reincarnation. Now it helps her to imagine that he has been reborn in another body and is learning lessons he didn't learn in his first life. However, she says, "It took seventeen years for the pain to get somewhere where I really didn't feel guilty and it wasn't so overwhelming."

Today, Shelly lives an emotionally and physically healthy life, but the story might not have ended so happily. In the 1999 movie *Valerie Flake*, the eponymous heroine indulges in risky behavior following her husband's death: promiscuous sex, heavy drinking, picking up hitchhikers. She is bitter and withdrawn and gives up a promising career as an artist to be a supermarket checker. Toward the movie's conclusion, we learn that she and her husband had quarreled before he took off in a rage on his motorcycle and crashed into a utility pole.

When it leads to dangerous behaviors, guilt can kill. A young man whose wife was murdered told Jennifer that he rode his motorcycle at high speeds without a helmet because he blamed himself for not replacing the lock on the back door as he'd promised he would. He began many of their sessions, "If only . . . "

Guilt can take other, less dramatic forms that can be just as lethal. "Forgetting" to buckle one's seatbelt; not finding the time to replace the bald tires on the car; not taking prescribed medication or seeking medical advice for unusual symptoms; eating or drinking too much; taking drugs—these may account, in part, for the higher mortality rate seen among the recently bereaved. One widow felt so stricken that she hadn't found her husband in time to rush him to the hospital after a heart attack—he had been mowing the lawn and collapsed—that she severely neglected her own health. Two years later, she, too, was dead.

Suicides and violent deaths are particularly guilt-inducing. Joan Nye, whose nineteen-year-old son, John, committed suicide, is still anguished that she didn't recognize the extent of her son's mental illness. Self-assured and involved in numerous activities during her own high school days, she couldn't comprehend John's inability to make friends or his sudden unwillingness to apply himself to his studies. "For me, growing up was fun and easy," she says. "Now I feel to blame for not understanding my son." When John dropped out of school a few weeks before graduation, she insisted, with his therapist's approval, that he get a job and an apartment—"tough love" methods that, she believes, were too tough for someone as sick as John.

Joan's road to healing has been long and hard, although she has gradually been able to forgive herself. "I'll always wish I could have helped him," she says, "but various mental health professionals hadn't been able to help him either."

After John died, she felt several kinds of relief—and guilt for feeling any relief at all. Added to the guilt was the burden of dealing with the stigma of suicide. One thing that has helped her is being able to see that John's suicide was a result of his mental illness, and she has begun to speak about it in order to raise awareness in her community. "As a parent, you want to take care of your child, so that's a source of shame, as well as the social stigma of suicide," she says. "We didn't mention suicide in John's obituary, but now I would say it, in order to spread awareness." It's still hard for her to tell people John was mentally ill; because he was so afraid of being crazy, she feels she's betraying him. But recognizing that in some ways her son was beyond anyone's reach has helped her feel less self-blame, and in sharing her experience, she has found healing.

When friends tell Kathy Brandt, whose newborn son Matthew died of a heart defect, that they feel sorry for her, she doesn't share her positive feelings regarding his short life. In fact, she doesn't talk about her relief with anyone except her husband. She thinks that, because the loss of a baby is considered so tragic, she might be thought kooky for talking about this response.

During her pregnancy, she and her husband Thane came to expect baffled looks when they told people they didn't intend to pursue a heart transplant for Matthew.

After numerous discussions with specialists, doing their own research, and seeking advice from Kathy's brother, a physician, they decided against the risky and painful operation. Even assuming an infant heart became available in time—a big assumption, with the scarcity of infant hearts—sentencing him to life as a cardiac cripple was unacceptable to them. "He would have lived not knowing if he'd make it through this cold, or pneumonia, or chickenpox. I couldn't imagine living like that," says Kathy. For many people, she believes, "a heart transplant sounds like an easy solution, but it's not." She's come to recognize that her perceptions and other people's are at odds—and that's fine. Because they kept Matthew's quality of life uppermost, she and Thane are satisfied that they made the right choice, and Matthew's peaceful death seemed to confirm it. She doesn't feel her friends would understand that, for her, Matthew's brief life was "a huge gift." "I feel luckier than a lot of people out there," she says.

When we began interviewing people for this book, we expected to find lots of guilt. We assumed, because relief is so taboo, that people would have problems both admitting it and living with it. Instead, we found a substantial number who felt no guilt at all. Our interview subjects were approximately evenly divided, with half feeling guilt and half feeling none. However, more of those from the "relationship relief" category reported feeling no guilt, whereas more from the "altruistic" and "dual" relief categories felt guilty. Jennifer and Chris fall into these categories themselves, with Jennifer, in the "relationship" category, having felt very little guilt, and Chris, in the "dual," quite a lot.

Although these results may seem counterintuitive, on closer examination they make sense. To an extent guilt is a function of love. When you love someone you want to do everything you can for him or her; a loved one's continuing illness and death feels, on some level, like a personal failure. Also because the person is so deeply loved, families feel they've betrayed him by wishing him gone. However, this being said, we wish to remind readers that, among our subjects, guilt or its absence was found in all three categories of relationships—not just the loving ones.

We believe that the lack of guilt we found shows that people are better at trusting their own responses than the experts think. It's possible, too, that those who contacted us, or agreed to an interview when we contacted them, have dealt successfully with their guilt and are ready to be more open, in at least a limited way.

Jennifer's story:

While I see now how deluded I was, I really believed that if we could only move to another, bigger town, where I could attend school, my marriage to Paul would improve. I thought that studying for a master's degree would fulfill me enough that I would mind his criticisms less. *Maybe he would even like me better*, I thought wistfully. I had loved studying nursing, but taking so much science, I had missed many other fascinating areas such as history, literature, and art.

Paul had built a reputation as a dedicated physician, and in those years he was heavily recruited by headhunters looking for good doctors. At least twice a month the phone rang with another query. While in medical school he had qualified for a government program that, in exchange for his agreeing to work for three years in a medically underserved area, paid his school loans; those three years were almost up. I couldn't wait.

We looked at two places I especially liked: Marietta, Ohio, and Cold Springs, New York. Both communities were genuinely welcoming, and Cold Springs was across the Hudson River from my mother's home. Both had the advantage of being much larger than where we were living, and I was filled with hope when I thought of moving.

But Paul, it turned out, was just going through the motions. He was making a six-figure income in our little town and had no desire to uproot his practice. His father, knowing how unhappy I was, sat him down and urged him to consider my feelings, too, but it had no effect I could discern.

His relationship with Elizabeth was getting strained as well, although I think Paul truly loved her and wanted her to love him. In public he tried to play the role of doting father, but he worked so much that it was me she turned to for comfort. When she was a year old, we attended a neighborhood barbecue one Sunday afternoon. Paul tried to cuddle her, but she stiffened and began to wail. Frustrated, he shook her. I was horrified. I recognized, as I hadn't before, that my marriage was over. I had been willing to set aside my own misery, but I wasn't willing to sacrifice my daughter, too. After that, I was afraid to leave her alone with him.

I still cringe when I think what it might have meant to divorce Paul—the custody arrangements, divided loyalties, and wrangling over money that seemed inevitable.

Although I initially felt guilty that I might have driven him to suicide, the medical examiner's ruling that he fell asleep at the wheel convinced me that I wasn't to blame. I felt very little guilt about my relief when Paul died. It made perfect sense to me to be relieved to be out of such a soul-killing marriage.

For a number of those who experienced "relationship relief," there was a sense of having paid their dues while the person was alive. Having been sufficiently threatened, humiliated, imprisoned, mistreated, and, in short, forced to give up so much, they feel nothing but relief now. What's more, they feel entitled to it. This doesn't necessarily mean they don't have lingering problems with anger or regret or unfinished business of some kind, but it does mean that they aren't dealing with guilt.

Some were fortunate enough to be absolved of all guilt by their dead. Fletcher Newby, whose wife, Elaine, died after a lifetime with rheumatoid arthritis, says, "I told my kids I have no guilt at all." Fletcher is happily remarried to a much younger woman and believes Elaine would approve. "My wonderful wife Elaine expected to die before me and told me to marry again. She felt I would be better off married. She felt married men are healthier, and she wanted me to be happy. I don't feel guilty because she insisted on it so many times."

Ken Nichols says that the way in which his mentally ill and sometimes violent wife, Eileen, killed herself in a foreign country made it easier for him to recover. Eileen took an overdose of pills while on a tour of Bali, and Ken didn't even have to travel there; his local funeral home made all the arrangements. She also left no guilt-inducing suicide note—another huge favor she did him, as Ken sees it. In fact, everything about her death was a gift to him. "Can you imagine the guilt if she had done it in our house, and I hadn't gotten home in time?" he asks. "My forgiveness came from her."

For others, the lack of guilt has been replaced by something more complicated. Edna Matthews married her husband, Gerald, because she was pregnant. "Nothing was ever good," she says of her fifty-seven-year marriage, but leaving him wasn't an option. "Where I came from, people just didn't get divorced," she says. Because she had no job skills, leaving her marriage "would have meant going home to live with my mother and hearing 'I told you so' for the rest of my life."

Nine years before his death, Gerald began having a series of small strokes. Irascible and demanding before the strokes, he became downright violent afterward. "His agitation just grew and grew," Edna says. "He would lash out at me, the furniture, the door that wouldn't open, anything. I was afraid of him all the time." Then he developed Parkinson's, too, and had to be put in a nursing home—a huge relief for her. "I thought, *Oh God, peace at last*," she says. One night, after three years there, he developed a fever and labored breathing, and the nursing home had him transported to the hospital. She remembers, "The nursing home gives you many opportunities to say what you want if you are very ill, and he had said he wanted everything done to keep him alive, everything. And I was praying, *Oh God, please don't let them look in his papers and find that.*" To her deep gratitude, he died before anyone could look for his advance directives.

She insists she had no guilt over her sense of freedom. She had been at the nursing home every single day. "I did everything I knew to do, that I thought a person in my position would be expected to do. I have a clean conscience."

But surprisingly, and distressingly, her conviction of having served her time has been a good news–bad news situation. "Before his death, I think there was some guilt because he was sick and I wasn't," she says. "But I haven't felt guilt, or maybe I haven't allowed myself to feel it, after his death, because I still think that I gave so much to keep the marriage going." Although during his illness Gerald was, in her words, "an insatiable, weird pit" she constantly had to amuse, feed, and tend to, since his death she has had a difficult time moving on. Her freedom to spend all day in bed if she chose turned into an inability to get out of bed, and her initial relief into an emptiness she cannot fill, although she denies that she misses anything about her husband or her life with him.

Feelings that surprise us—and guilt, like any emotion, can descend without warning—are particularly difficult to cope with. It's entirely possible to expect to feel only relieved—or only grief-stricken—and find yourself caught off-guard by the opposite feeling or more of a mix than you expected. You find yourself trying to overrule your heart with your head. *But he was my father! Why don't I feel sadder?* you wonder. Or conversely, *He was so cold and uncaring! I can't understand why I miss him so much.* This was Jennifer's experience after her father's death. Although her parents had divorced when she was seven, and throughout the years her father was only a distant presence in her life, when he died of Alzheimer's in February 2002 she was surprised at the depth of her grief. "I lost any hope of a true connection with the man I called Dad," she says. "I wept for what never was, and now, never could be."

Karen Cox, by contrast, has never looked back. When her mother, Josefina, died of breast cancer, she says, "She did her death like she did her life, closed her eyes and didn't let anyone in. I always had the feeling that she could have at least tugged at my hand, or something. But she didn't."

Josefina's last rejection, as she was dying, was typical of the way she treated Karen throughout her life. "I was hoping this time would be different. I always kept hoping," Karen says. Particularly painful afterward was hearing her mother's friends and relatives rave about her. "For her wake, I invited a ton of her friends," says Karen. "She was seventy-seven, very outgoing, played tennis, and all her tennis friends were there. It was a party." Josefina had some cousins on the East Coast who also shared fond memories of her. "They talked about how wonderful she was, how they still miss her," says Karen. Her voice grows sad as she continues, "how beautiful she was, her sense of humor . . . I never saw it."

Karen's relief at her mother's death was boundless—
and guilt-free. In fact, she was stunned by her lack of regret of any kind. She says, "I feel guilt for other things,
but not for this. It's just not an issue, and in a way it's so
wonderful, it's as if there's no place for it to land, no place
for it to hook onto inside of me. It's so freeing. There
aren't that many things that flow through you so easily."

She vividly remembers eating dinner with her husband, Greg, whom her mother had always disparaged,
two hours after Josefina had died. "We went to a Mexican
restaurant, and I'll never forget how good it tasted—
omigod, it really did," she says. Greg, who had seen her
struggle with the relationship for so many years, knew
how she felt. "I didn't have to put it into words," says
Karen.

Something she is grateful for every year is that "on
Mother's Day, I don't have to go find a card that is carefully worded, that expresses the love, and yet the sheer
frustration and agony that comes from trying to be close to
someone that won't allow you to be close." Over the years,
scouring the racks for the right card became emblematic of
the hopelessness of the relationship. "Yet I always loved
her," Karen says. "She just couldn't give me love."

Karen's reaction came as a wonderfully pleasant surprise to her, but not everyone will be so fortunate. You
may feel isolated, because people feel awkward in the
presence of the newly bereaved and now avoid you. As a
relieved griever, you may feel doubly isolated, believing
others wouldn't understand your reaction anyway.

Just as those who are angry at the dead may need to
forgive them, those carrying a load of guilt need to for-

give themselves. As Celia Schroeder discovered, the validation of others—in her case, other Alzheimer's spouses who reminded her how terrible the disease was and how they, too, wished for the end—helped her do this. Support groups, formal and informal, are great sources of help, and we recommend them highly. Even a support group of one is helpful. "It's not uncommon for people to stop to talk to me when they see me out in the community," says Karen Krissovich, a hospice nurse. "There is a need to process the experience with someone who can understand what the dying was like, and validate that everything possible was done in the name of comfort, and that the decisions they made were correct." At the other end of the spectrum, hospice nurse Donna Bueti says, "I can think of a number of families where the person was hard to get along with. One specifically had been hard to deal with before his illness, and very self-absorbed. He ended up with a brain tumor and his behavior became completely unmanageable in the home. His aggressiveness toward other people included peeing on their shoes when they stood him up, and hitting them. And I think his estranged wife, as well as the sister and brother-in-law involved in his care, very openly expressed relief at his final passing, because he wasn't an elderly fellow. He took a while to die." When this family has to deal with any lingering guilt feelings, Donna, an impartial observer, is able to remind them of what she saw.

Gloria Reed, whose husband Nick died of an epileptic seizure, berated herself for staying away from him after he abused her and her son. She was helped greatly by a police officer who reminded her after Nick's death that it would have been too dangerous to stay in her home. She was also helped by her minister, who told her it made sense to be relieved to be out of an abusive marriage. Without accurate information, or the corroboration of others, our imaginations tend to run wild, fueling our guilt.

Many people find that guilt is part of the recovery process and dissipates with time. Therese Rando writes, "It is a cruel trick of human nature that, in the early phases of mourning, in contrast to the way the deceased is remembered, individuals tend to recall everything negative on their part in the relationship, and fail to remember their more positive contributions." If you picked up this book because you are troubled by guilt feelings, maybe thinking of guilt as a temporary trick of human nature will help. However, because you are the only one who knows the degree to which guilt is interfering with your life, you are the only one who knows whether you need a therapist. If some time has elapsed since your loss, and you feel very isolated by lack of family or community support, you may need to explore your emotional state further with a therapist who has some background with bereavement and transition issues. Both Jennifer and Chris were helped immeasurably at different times by those we paid to listen to us. There's something "clean" about letting all your feelings out to someone who has no agenda, because your friends, well-meaning though they are, will have their own reactions regarding your dead that don't necessarily line up with yours. Sometimes, an impartial therapist can make us see how inappropriate our self-blame is and that, no matter how many times we wished for a death, we aren't all-powerful and didn't cause it. Jennifer saw a young woman in her practice who felt guilty that she didn't feel sadder after her father's death. "I should have tried harder to get to know him," she wept. "Now it's too late!" Using a type of rational-emotive therapy, Jennifer challenged the client to examine her relationship with her father and helped her dispute some of her beliefs about it. "How often did your dad call you?" Jennifer asked. The woman admitted that, although she tried to call him every other month, her father rarely returned her calls, never acknowledged her birthday or holidays, and didn't attend her wedding. "I was just a little girl when he left us," she said. "He stopped writing and calling after he remarried and started a new family." Gradually, she began to recognize that her father, an adult, bore the greater responsibility for their lack of contact, and she began to reframe her self-blame as regret. "I wish it could have been different," she told Jennifer eventually. This woman still feels sadness, but she has much less guilt.

Jennifer sometimes uses a technique known as "guilt-free day" with her clients. By giving clients permission to choose an alternative to the way they've been coping, she helps them regain some control over their thoughts and feelings. Also, guilt can become so ingrained that it becomes a habit rather than a true emotion. On a guilt-free day, you practice becoming aware of what generates your guilt feelings and rejecting feelings of culpability. You may have to remind yourself many times during the day that you are taking a vacation from guilt and that you deserve to enjoy one day without any emotional static. At the end of the day, ask yourself: *How does guilt-free living feel?* Do you notice a change in your energy level? Do you like the sensation enough to try it again? You may decide to adopt guilt-free living as a new habit.

Paradoxically, forcing yourself to feel only guilt for an hour a day can also help banish it. If you begin to think of more pleasant topics, immediately switch back to guilt; remind yourself those pleasant thoughts will have to wait till later. This technique, like the guilt-free day, reinforces your sense of control. You also give yourself permission to act differently.

Because each client is different, therapists use various methods to treat guilt. Some find that "empty-chair work," which brings the past into the present, is therapeutic. The client pretends that the dead person is sitting across from her and talks to him or her, thus helping to resolve guilt. Some recommend journaling about your feelings. In some cases, writing a letter to the dead person helps. Any or all of these techniques may move you further along the road to healing.

It makes sense to reach out for help if you feel you need it, if only to feel less alone. Being able to talk—and talk and talk and talk—your experience through with a neutral listener can be healing. It doesn't mean you're sick, or that something's terribly wrong with you. You'd go to the doctor if you had a nagging physical problem; the same is true for a psychological one. "I think anyone who thinks they should seek counseling, should," says Ken Doka, consultant to the Hospice Foundation of America. We concur.

If you live in a small town and prefer to keep your secret, strangers can make the best friends—and the huge popularity of online chat rooms and bulletin boards testifies to the efficacy of talking to others—anonymously—who can identify with your situation. At the bereavement site we visited, others expressed great compassion for our fictional "nontraditional widow" and shared stories of their own. At a number of bereavement sites, you can join in a discussion with others who also had difficult relationships with their dead. The Internet can be a source of facts as well—about grief, guilt, forgiveness, anger, and a multitude of other related topics.

For reasons that aren't clear, loss sometimes leads, temporarily, to lower self-esteem. Guilt certainly lowers self-esteem. You may be more prone to feelings of guilt because you're feeling less sure of yourself and your new roles. You may even feel you deserve to feel guilty. As Dick Appling found, getting busy is a good way to boost self-esteem. Whatever you accomplish, especially if it involves helping others, can make you feel more in control. Treating yourself well by eating healthy meals, getting enough sleep, and doing some form of physical activity can boost endorphin levels, those feel-good chemicals that make you feel more at peace with the world.

"Guilt is such a useless emotion," one widow complained, referring to the irrational guilt that can follow a death. "All it does is make you feel terrible. It doesn't point you in any direction." However, none of us would want to get rid of appropriate guilt, which keeps us moral and law-abiding. However, even inappropriate guilt tells us something about ourselves, even if it's something we don't particularly want to hear. Maybe guilt feels safer than admitting our own powerlessness over a random, and often perversely cruel, universe. Guilt, too, reminds us of our humanness, our perfect imperfection. Tell yourself you did the best you could with what you knew at the time. It's certainly true.

The ideas we've suggested here may help you, but you are unique in what you brought to your loss situation and you may be dealing with more than just the shame and guilt of a relief death. If you were raised to be a perfectionist; if you have had emotional problems or clinical depression in the past; if your family or social circle is particularly judgmental and unsupportive; if you feel very isolated; if your guilt has stayed longer than you think it should have—these are all signs that you may need more in-depth help. Don't be afraid to ask for it.

6

Social Support

"Isolation is the sum total of wretchedness to man."
— Thomas Carlyle

Maybe the only thing harder than having a nontraditional response is not being able to talk about it. If there's one thing grief studies agree on, it is that human beings, as social animals, need to feel they are not alone. Jennifer was once asked if she had a support group for "those who were grieving sons of bitches"! We all need to feel understood and appreciated, to connect in positive ways, especially when raging emotions threaten to swamp us.

Poor social support can be a red flag to grief recovery. In fact, in recent years social isolation has been associated with a higher risk of mortality, not only among the bereaved but also among the elderly in general. One theory as to why widowers are more likely to die after the death of their wives is that the marital relationship, for many men, is the only close relationship they have. Widows fare better because they tend to reach out to each other and band together for support. Social support isn't just desirable; it's a matter of life and death. It's particularly ironic that relieved grievers, when most in need of comfort and understanding, can find themselves further stressed by ostracism, whether perceived or real.

Jennifer's story:

The news of Paul's death shot through our little town like a bolt of lightning. At daybreak, townspeople began knocking on the front door, their arms loaded with biscuits, coffee, hams, donuts, flowers, and beautiful fruit baskets. Most had tears streaming down their faces. Their beloved doctor and friend had died during the night, and they gathered at my home to express their feelings of grief and disbelief. I understood; but more than anything I needed to be alone with my baby daughter to process this shocking event. Irrationally, even though I was planning to leave him, I was angry at Paul for leaving me, and I vacillated between fury, overwhelming sadness at the death of a man I had once loved, and relief that my marriage was over.

It says something about the esteem in which Paul was held that the mayor ordered all flags in Lancaster County lowered to half-mast. Sympathy cards clogged the mailbox. In a custom that seems quaint now, but is still widely practiced in the rural South, townspeople draped my door with swaths of black crepe. The community offered to start a scholarship fund for Elizabeth.

People arrived at the house in droves. The situation was more than a little bizarre for me. These kind people needed consolation, and they looked to me to share their sorrow, but I was the last person who should have been asked to do this. Comforting them meant acting out a lie. Thank God, my mother, a Southern lady in the best sense of the word, was there to help me. She knew some things about my life with Paul, because I had told her, but her relationship with him was more like everyone else's. She was the essence of Southern hospitality in those early days and rescued me.

Paul's closest friend, David, knew of Paul's depression, and he was the one I called first, after leaving the emergency room. The next day, he went with me to retrace the accident and try to make some sense of what had happened. David's support was very helpful, but his genuine despair at the death of his friend meant I couldn't share my feelings of liberation with him.

Certain moments remain vivid. Upstairs, helping my sisters, who had come for the funeral, unpack, I could say things like, "I'm moving to Hawaii," and they'd laughingly help me plan my future life. On my way back downstairs to receive yet another sad visitor, I would carefully rearrange my face to that of grieving widow.

There were several memorial services for Paul in the following days. At one, I sat between my sisters and listened to the minister, a pompous good-old boy Paul had loathed, describe my husband in glowing terms. *Paul would have been furious*, I thought. The whole situation struck me as so improbable that I started to giggle. I could only hope that those sitting behind me mistook my shaking shoulders for sobs.

So I had degrees of social support, with only a few people, mostly my family, knowing about "the real Paul," with the majority knowing nothing. The irony was that the town could have given me terrific support had I been truly grief-stricken. Poor people, they had no way of knowing how conflicted they made me feel. I knew that there was no point in trying to tell anyone what Paul had really been like. I recognized that wanting to tell them the truth was a purely selfish impulse, and I might not have been believed anyway. Besides, what would it matter? Paul was dead now, and it was up to me to make sense of his death in my own way.

Of those we interviewed, some were fortunate in having good social support; some, like Jennifer, had limited or inappropriate support, and a few poor souls had none.

When the community has witnessed a lingering illness from start to finish, support is likely to be strong and very appropriate. The loss has been public, and others have a sense of having shared the family's suffering. "Thanks for being such a wonderful wife to Don!" Don's sister told Chris at his funeral, and when Chris expressed doubts to her sister Carol as to whether she, Chris, had done enough for Don, Carol hugged her, saying, "You did, you did, you did!" She and her children were inundated with condolence cards, and a man who owned an insurance agency, and with whom Don had worked, started a memorial scholarship through one of the state's universities. And even though the expressions of sympathy didn't overtly acknowledge the relief she was feeling, others' awareness that she had suffered, as well as her husband, was helpful and affirming.

For Chris, others' memories, shared at his funeral and in condolence cards and visits, of Don's sense of humor, creativity, compassion, and strong sense of business ethics were uniquely comforting. Although they made her cry, they were testimony to the fact that his life, despite his five isolated years in the nursing home, had touched many others. Others' reminiscences reminded Chris that the vicious disease that killed her husband couldn't touch his spirit.

Social participation was especially valuable for the family of an eleven-year-old girl, Maria, who developed a neurological illness at age three that even the most eminent specialists could not diagnose. The family became well known in the community, thanks in part to the mysterious nature of her illness; every few years, the local newspaper ran an article on the theme of "What's Wrong with Maria?" Each Halloween, Maria's mother dressed her daughter as a princess and wheeled her around the neighborhood. Although the family could easily have isolated itself, they chose instead to try to demystify Maria's disability; ultimately, as she was dying, they encouraged everyone to participate in her journey out of life.

Maria was able to attend school with the help of an aide and a sign-language interpreter, but as her short life wound to a close toward the end of fifth grade, the family took her out of school and called hospice in. Maria's parents went out of their way to make her classmates, who were told she was dying, welcome in their home, and the school cooperated by allowing several of them each day to visit her. Although by this time Maria was paralyzed, had to be fed with a feeding tube, and could not speak, the children read to her and did origami for her, as well as spoke to her in sign language. Neighborhood parents volunteered to stay with her so that her parents could get away occasionally for an evening.

At her funeral, Maria was dressed in the princess costume she loved, and her parents showed a video of her life so that school friends would not be frightened by the sight of Maria in her casket. At the graveside ceremony, attended by many, pink and purple balloons were released into the sky.

"The whole community felt sadness and relief," a neighbor reflected afterward. "And the whole community gave permission for the relief. People had seen her not have quality of life for so long. She couldn't play, she couldn't be a child, she was in pain. But she touched so many people. . . ." We couldn't help but be impressed that this child's parents, through their courage and generosity, were able to teach a great many people, children especially, that the quality of a life has nothing to do with its length.

The death of a child evokes great sympathy in our culture; even with the relief element, it is a particularly *enfranchised* loss. A person with a nontraditional loss response, however, is *disenfranchised* from both the existence and the expression of certain reactions—emotional, intellectual, social, and spiritual. Charles Corr writes, "How many times have grieving persons been told: 'Don't feel that way'; 'Try not to think those thoughts'; 'Don't say those things' (about God, or the doctor, or the person who caused the death); 'You shouldn't act like that just because someone you loved died.'" Corr describes this phenomenon as "oppressive toleration," which sends grievers the message that they must keep certain grief reactions private "in order not to trouble or disturb others by bringing it out in the open, or expressing it in certain ways."

"Hero worship" is often a factor in these situations, whether the hero is the deceased, as in Jennifer's case, or the survivor, as with Marla Mabry, mother of a severely handicapped girl. When the dead person is idealized, like Paul, you can't tell the truth about him; when the survivor is idealized, as Marla felt she was, you can't tell the truth about the relationship. Unlike Maria, Marla's daughter Tiffany was not sick and not obviously suffering; for Marla to have expressed relief at her daughter's death would have been, Marla felt, taboo.

Both kinds of hero worship are equally effective at shutting people's mouths. The events of September 11, 2001, created thousands of heroes by dint of the way they died. We believe that at least some of them left relief in their wake, and we wonder if those survivors will ever be able to talk about it. We doubt they will be able to do so publicly, at least for a long while.

Leave it to *Doonesbury* cartoonist Garry Trudeau to rush in where angels fear to tread. Within a month of the terrorist attack, he had Mike Doonesbury flying to New York to attend the funeral of "Mr. Bellows," a former boss, and now one of the World Trade Center victims. We see Mike with Marcia, a former coworker, sitting in the pew of a church, talking about Bellows. Mike admits he feels "uncomfortable" to be there, whereupon Marcia tells him that Bellows died a hero, helping others out of the building, and Mike amends that to "mortified." In the next strip, Mike admits that he thought Bellows was "the most unprincipled person I've ever known," and Marcia replies that yes, in light of his heroism she almost regrets her sexual harassment suit against him. So much for heroes, Trudeau seems to be saying.

As part of our research, we visited an Internet chat room for widowed people to see if anyone there had experienced a relief death. The responses surprised us—both the willingness to tell all, as well as the compassion chat-room visitors expressed for each other. One woman—we'll call her Melanie—described being so filled with rage at her dead husband that she was expelled from a bereavement support group in her town. The other members of the group, Melanie said, were too uncomfortable around her, and the group leader suggested she "needed more in-depth counseling" than the group could provide. Even one of her close friends, a social worker, confided that she worried because Melanie didn't feel enough guilt about her feelings of relief. Another woman told of being married to an emotionally abusive man who had advanced cirrhosis of the liver due to alcoholism. However, before he could die of that malady, he was strangled by an inmate at the prison where he worked. Now his coworkers consider him a hero, and she finds herself in the strange and uncomfortable role of hero's wife. She is furious that death has bestowed on her husband a halo he didn't earn. She is able to tell few people about the situation she's in. She keeps her thoughts to herself, concentrates on recovering, and is determined to make a better choice next time.

The second woman was getting plenty of social support, but, as in Jennifer's case, it was inappropriate. It's questionable whether inappropriate support is better than none, or whether it makes a painful situation worse. Hearing how wonderful someone was, when you are trying to come to terms with your own, very different, knowledge of who they were, is far from comforting—yet many of those we interviewed found themselves in this predicament. The numerous visits and phone calls after Paul's death made Jennifer aware of the gulf between her private self and the self she had to be in public. In her private world, she felt lonely and isolated.

She even gave up answering the phone for several days because, with adjusting to Paul's death already so difficult, the added burden of keeping up the grieving-widow facade became an overwhelming burden. In addition, she began to fear that responding to others' sadness by sharing her own might cause the dam to break and that she would end up talking about the awfulness of her marriage. She decided it was safer to avoid those situations entirely and got in the habit of mentally reaching for her mask when she had to go out in public.

Chris's parish priest told her that the Irish had a subtle way of acknowledging a problem relationship that preceded a death: "I'm sorry for your troubles." This lovely phrase, he said, covered all kinds of situations admirably. Some of the widows we interviewed have a similar insight because of their own marriages. Lenore Lansing, whose jealous, possessive husband dictated her every move, reflects, "When my circle of friends comes to me and says, 'Oh, can you believe they got a divorce?' I always say, 'You never know what goes on behind closed doors. You just don't know whose fault it is.'" She is realistic as to which of them, she or her husband, was the more admired in their small town. "If I had ever divorced my husband, I know who they would've blamed it on," she says, "and it wouldn't have been him, because he was so well thought of in the community."

Within a year of Ed's death she moved to a larger town where no one knew her or her husband. "The people we were closest to in the community we lived in, I have nothing to do with them anymore," she says. "One of them calls every once in a while and sometimes I don't even take the call. I'd rather not have to listen to how wonderful he was. I'm just not ready for that." With two of her close friends, and her two children, she can be honest. "With them, I can say how great he was for the community," she says grimly. "In fact, he gave so much to everyone else that there was nothing left. We got the short end of the stick."

For Lenore, moving away has been good in some ways, bad in others. "There are expectations from the family that I should be feeling differently than I am," she says. "I've gotten pretty blunt with both my husband's brother and sister. Because they can feel any way they want, but I don't have to feel that way, and I don't feel that way." Her attitude hasn't discouraged them from calling; in fact, "I'm grateful to be so far away from them, otherwise they could appear on my doorstep."

Yet she fights loneliness and depression, using unhealthy eating to—maybe literally—fill the void. Another widow, Edna Matthews, has also been plagued with depression. After her husband, Gerald, died of a stroke, she felt no guilt, only "a sense of freedom, that a big burden had been lifted off of me." However, she has been dismayed at her inability to find new activities to replace her intensive caregiving duties. "I thought that the day he died, and I had all of that behind me, I would be out tripping the light fantastic and having a lot of fun." Instead, she says ruefully, "I have a totally undirected, unfulfilling, unscheduled life—which a lot of people would say is great," she says. "But it's not." She quit the symphony chorale, which she used to enjoy, and has been unable to find new interests to replace it. "I never thought it would happen," she puzzles. "I don't think the joy went out of the music; I think the joy went out of my attitude."

One of the hazards of lying to others is having to lie to yourself, too, thus losing touch with your own needs and wants; maybe this is what happened to Edna and Lenore. Kathy Charmaz, professor of sociology at Sonoma State University, believes that what we grieve after a death is the part of ourselves that interacted with that person—the part of us that was "activated" by him or her. If we loved him, and loved who we were in his presence, the loss of that aspect of ourselves is deep and searing. If he was someone we feared and despised, the absence left afterward is harder to define. If, like Lenore, we became used to "shutting down" in the person's presence, we may be left with a gaping hole we can't begin to know how to fill because it's been part of our psyche for so long.

Like Lenore, relieved grievers are denied the remedy that works best: telling and retelling their stories. Talking about your loss, and sorting out your reactions in the presence of another person, make it real. One of the surprises for us in writing this book was that several people approached us asking to be interviewed—two of them nearly begging us to do so. They confided that we were the only ones ever to hear the truth.

Neither were they simply hungry for someone to listen; seeing the printed transcript of their interviews was a powerful affirmation as well. One woman took her transcript to Thanksgiving dinner and read it aloud to her grown children, giving them, for the first time, a glimpse into what her life with their father had been like. In this way, she was able to enter into an honest conversation with them about her ambivalence surrounding his death, as well as the choices she was contemplating now. Another made copies to share with her friends, who had only a vague knowledge of her abusive marriage.

Another widow, Evelyn Washburn, who had to listen to others sing the praises of her privately abusive husband, Mike, called Jennifer five times with additional information that occurred to her in the days following the interview. Like Lenore and Edna, Evelyn has had a difficult time finding direction in life since Mike's death. However, Jennifer noticed that with each call she seemed to gain new insight into her unhappy marriage and clarity about the future. During their last conversation, she told Jennifer she had decided to return to school to study computer programming and didn't think she'd need to call her anymore.

Unintentionally, we became the repositories for some deep, dark secrets. To be a relieved griever is to be a keeper of secrets—a lonely place. When, for her dissertation, Jennifer was interviewing spouses who had lost a mate to cancer, a dapper older man confided that his marriage, widely admired as ideal, had actually been "a forty-year private hell." He still had nightmares, he said, that his wife might return, vampirelike, to haunt him. He told Jennifer that, as he sat listening to the minister intone falsehoods about his wife, the song going through his head was "Ding, Dong, the Witch Is Dead." A young woman whose grandfather had sexually abused her found herself humming, instead of funeral hymns, AC-DC's "Highway to Hell."

Even if the relief might have been endorsed, say, in the case of a long, debilitating illness, grievers were discreet about who they shared it with. "It's real personal," says Adele Bachmann, whose mother died after a medical mishap rendered her an invalid for sixteen years. "I have no desire to talk to strangers about it. You [the authors] are the odd exception because you are focused on the subject, but it makes most people really uncomfortable, because they don't know what to say."

We all fear others' censure, especially in the vulnerable state loss throws us into. Chris remembers, in those early months, feeling as though a layer of her skin had been peeled off, leaving her ultrasensitive to slights, comments, and conversational nuances she ordinarily wouldn't have noticed. Expressing a nonsanctioned emotion feels too risky. "Some people just didn't understand. They thought it sounded cold and callous to feel relief," said a woman whose mother died of a series of strokes.

In particular, as some widows found, the combination of small town and social prominence made for a tight fit—

and a very uneasy one at that. Evelyn Washburn, whose interview with Jennifer proved a turning point for her, met her husband when she was still a teenager. Although they dated for two years, she missed the signs of Mike's excessive drinking and its disastrous effects on his personality. She suspects that Mike was probably a functioning alcoholic even then but took pains to conceal it until after they were married. There was always a lot of alcohol at family gatherings, so socializing usually meant a confrontation when he and Evelyn got home. His favorite way of expressing his displeasure with her was throwing things—the phone, suitcases, shoes, plates of food. Sometimes he threw Evelyn; when she was lucky, she landed on a bed or a sofa. At night, she'd listen for his footsteps on the stairs, stomach in knots, wondering what awaited her and her older son—he favored the younger one—when he came in from his job managing a bar and supper club.

Leaving Mike wasn't an option. "Mike kept promising things would get better," she says. "And if he hadn't died, I probably would still be married, trying to keep things together." Divorcing him, she believed, would have felt like the ultimate failure, "like I couldn't even be married and stay married."

Mike's job made him well known in their small town, and at work he had an uncanny ability to turn on the charm and play the genial host. That, as well as his large extended family, made for a very public life and death. When he died of a heart attack at forty-nine, townspeople packed the church as well as the graveside service. "It was very hard to juggle my feelings in such a public place," Evelyn says. "Of course, nobody knew about the situation in my house. I had to pretend to be the grieving widow."

Hearing how great Mike was has been a trial for Evelyn and her older son, Jared, whom Mike also abused. For months, people encountering her or Jared would regale them with stories of Mike's antics at the restaurant and his outrageous sense of humor. "Jared tells me he's tired of hearing how terrific his dad was," says Evelyn. "People mean well, but they don't know what happened."

Evelyn avoids Mike's family now and doesn't attend their gatherings. When she does encounter someone who thinks her husband was Mr. Congeniality, she thinks to herself, "You didn't know him. If you'd stayed with me one night, you'd have seen what it was like."

Understandably, she has no interest in remarrying, although she has chosen to stay in their town. After all, she's used to lying. "Jared and I would lie to keep Mike from hurting us. I'd lie to his family, and my family, and people who knew us. We had to lie to stay safe." Evelyn still lies to stay safe—from the skepticism and criticism of others. She hopes that time will erase people's memories of her husband and that someday she'll be truly free of him.

Not everyone is capable of handling the clash between public and private reality so capably. A hospice nurse recounted a story of one of her clients who went to pieces at her husband's funeral. Previous to his illness, the woman, whom we'll call Arlene, had finally gathered up the courage to leave her abusive husband. When he was diagnosed with severe diabetes, Arlene felt too guilty to leave him, and though she did move him to a nursing home, she stayed in the marriage despite his continuing abusiveness. "She had symptoms of depression while he was dying," the hospice nurse told us, "but all we heard from her was how sick he was. She never talked about how cruel he was." At the funeral, his children, Arlene's stepchildren, spoke of what a caring father he was and how much he'd loved them. They ignored Arlene, whose quiet sobbing escalated to hysterical shrieks as she listened to their loving tributes. The hospice nurse stayed after the funeral to try to calm Arlene. "She was truly grieving him, even though he had abused her," the nurse told us. "And she had almost no support. Her friends didn't think she should be grieving. They kept saying, 'What's wrong? We thought you were going to divorce him.' She couldn't work, couldn't do much of anything, she was so depressed." The combination of grief, anger, and relief proved a volatile mix that was too much for Arlene to handle alone. She entered treatment for depression.

Beth Durkee, whose mother-in-law died of stomach cancer, felt outraged that people didn't know the Ann she knew—the jealous, petty, vengeful one. "I was terrible reading her obituary, I snorted and scoffed," Beth says. "The part about her coming to the Lord, well, that woman never mentioned the word 'God' to me in the entire time I knew her, and then all of a sudden, she's born again, comes to the Lord, blah, blah, blah. Give me a break! I don't think she even went to church in the thirteen years I knew her and all of a sudden, she's some kind of wonderful Christian." A Christian would have treated her better, to Beth's way of thinking.

Ann's funeral, in Beth's mind, rivaled Princess Diana's for pomp. "She had more bouquets than I could count, she had five ministers conducting the service. It was filled with all this grand and glorious music, which she had planned beforehand," Beth remembers. "I sat in front, which was good, because I was afraid people would be watching us for tears." From Beth, there were none. She simply felt vacant.

Beth can talk to her husband, Allen, about her feelings toward Ann, but he's the only one. "Some people really loved her," Beth acknowledges. "I was alone in my experience of her. I'm sure she aggravated other people, but I don't know about them, and the rest of the family didn't have my experience. So I'm the black sheep." Feeling lonely in a crowd is a lonely experience indeed.

Although grief therapists and bereavement literature consistently warn against moving within a year after a death, for some we interviewed it was an act of survival. Jennifer, claustrophobic in her small town before Paul's death, put the house up for sale within a few months and moved, as she had wanted to for years, to a town with a university where she could study for a master's degree. There she met her second husband and moved even farther away, to Montana. Those who move by themselves, like Lenore Lansing, may be in for a more difficult adjustment. A new community that doesn't know one's past is a mixed blessing. After a traditional loss, supportive friends and relatives can offer affirmation and encouragement to the newly bereaved who are struggling to adopt new roles and interests. But in the case of nontraditional loss, uncomprehending and/or unsupportive acquaintances can't or won't—or at least that's what the relieved griever thinks. Ironically, this might not be true, but they're never given the chance.

It's a peculiarly American wish to try to escape the past—and to fail. One widow, Meredith, moved away after her husband's death, putting as much distance as possible between her and her husband's family, who never knew, or chose to deny, his true character. However, she still has to deal with her husband's parents, who call weekly to talk to their two grandchildren, Erica and Christopher, and visit once each year. Because they were so young when he died, the children have few memories of their father, and their grandparents are only too eager to tell the children how marvelous he was. And though their blindness troubles her, Meredith works at maintaining a cordial relationship with them for the sake of her children. She resents it, but she keeps the secret, because she wants the same thing her in-laws do: her children's happiness. Maybe someday, she thinks, when the kids are older, she'll try to give them a more realistic picture of their dad. Then again, maybe she won't.

To her chagrin, Gloria Reed's younger son, T.J., whom Nick always favored over her older boy, Todd, still worships his dead stepfather. He insists on keeping Nick's baseball trophies in his room and has announced to his mother that when he grows up he intends to dye his hair black, like Nick's. He's even told her that he plans to take Nick's last name. Gloria bites her tongue for now and prays that T.J.'s memories will fade with time.

Sociologist Monica McGoldrick, associate professor at the Robert Wood Johnson Medical School in Piscataway,

New Jersey, and author of several books on troubled family relationships, believes that keeping secrets, particularly in abuse cases, is a bad idea. "The reason behind not telling about the abuse usually has to do with the sense that they were to blame in the first place; in other words, 'If I had been stronger, I would not have tolerated the abuse,'" she says. McGoldrick feels that telling the truth is very important, because it empowers others to do so, too. She doesn't accept the argument that just because the husband is dead the past no longer matters. "It doesn't matter that he's dead," she says. "He is still intimidating her with his power, even now." She suggests telling a few people who would be supportive, then gradually becoming more open about it. "She will be a shadow of herself if she doesn't tell," McGoldrick says. "It is never going to go away. It will always have happened."

For at least one brave woman, honesty has had its rewards. Regarding her bedridden mother she says, "I had not made a secret of the fact that our relationship was not good, or a secret of the fact that I didn't think she was a nice person." When people offered condolences after her death, she told them, "Please look at it, with me, as a major transition, not a major loss." She got mixed reactions. "Some people couldn't stop themselves from the automatic, 'I'm so sorry,'" she says. "And other people said, 'Thank you very much for saying that, because it frees me to say it.'"

Because women tend to be caregivers, the men in their lives may be blind to the costs exacted by an ill or disabled family member. Marla Mabry has never been able to tell her husband, Mark, how relieved she feels to no longer be caring for their seriously handicapped daughter, Tiffany. From the very beginning they saw their daughter differently. "That first year after Tiffany was born, I would tell my mother the things she wasn't doing because I didn't want to hide anything from her," says Marla. "Plus, it was a way for me to say those things aloud. I sure couldn't say them to Mark." His point of view was miles from hers. "I'd listen to Mark talking to his mother, and I'd hear him say, 'We just need to give her time.'" Marla has always prided herself on being a person who faces things squarely and deals with them realistically. "I had worked with parents of handicapped kids, and I knew there were people I didn't want to be like. I had seen people who were so unrealistic about their children. I wanted other kids to be able to accept Tiffany for what she was."

The day of Tiffany's funeral had some unexpectedly joyful moments for Marla. She was especially comforted by her daughter's final resting place. "Tiffany was buried in the cemetery where my dad and some of my aunts and uncles are, and you can stand and look out across a valley where I was raised," she says. After the funeral, Marla's brother, who owns a ranch nearby, told her he had a mare ready to foal. That afternoon, Marla and her family walked over the hill to her brother's place, where a new foal tottered unsteadily. "My brother had said, 'If it's a filly we'll name it Tiffany,'" Marla says, wiping her eyes. "So it wasn't a bad day, but Mark kept saying, 'This is the worst day of my life.'"

Marla knows that she will never be able to talk to her husband about Tiffany, and it's only one example of the distance between them. She was able to pour out her heart to her mother, who had been a caregiver for Marla's dad, and understood. Intentionally or not, Mark's attitude effectively relieved him of providing his wife emotional support.

Other families have been pleasantly surprised to find themselves able to speak openly among themselves about the oppression they could never verbalize when the person was alive. One woman told us, "My whole family gathered at my brother's house after my father died. One of the enlightening things was that, when we were all around the table, Dad's chair was there, and I think it was me who said, 'Now that Dad's dead, we can talk about all this stuff, and not have anybody tell us we're stupid.' We could talk about what a son of a bitch he was and how mean he was. It was really a revelation to us. We all laughed."

7

Unfinished Business

"Death ends a life, but not relationships, which struggle
on in the survivor's mind toward some resolution which
they may never find."

—Robert Anderson,
I Never Sang for My Father

To outsiders, Nicole Richardson's life looked perfect.
"There are pictures in the family album that could
have gone on any poster," she says. Nicole, her older
brother, Billy, younger brother, Buster, and her parents
lived in a succession of spacious homes in tony neighbor-
hoods. They drove late-model cars and dressed well. But
the household's emotional atmosphere was as cold as the
exterior was happy. Nicole believes now, after years of
therapy, that her family was narcissistic. In these families,
she explains, "The only requirement is that the children
be a reflection of the adults. So we didn't really exist as
who we were. We had no rights, and no ability to express

individuality." As long as she looked pretty and kept quiet, nothing else was required of her.

Although Nicole was emotionally abused, it was a subtle kind of abuse, with scars left on her soul, rather than on her skin. "The incidents I recall seem so ordinary, one by one," she admits. "It was the accumulation." A bright girl, she wasn't allowed to read Nancy Drew mysteries "or any of the fun stuff, like comics. My parents would go out and buy books that had medallions on them, and they'd say, 'This is the year's best book.' And that was what we were allowed to read."

Birthday and Christmas gifts were chosen to reflect her parents' impeccable taste. Her father's job as a pharmaceutical salesman allowed her mother to buy expensive furniture, which "was more important than the people," Nicole recalls. "So there was no food in the living room or anywhere but the kitchen, no feet on the table, no putting anything anywhere." Even in her bedroom, the furniture, with its ornate curlicues and fragile finish, permitted no childish exuberance. "If you put a glass on it, it left a ring that was permanent, so you couldn't do anything on this furniture." To her everlasting disappointment, she got more of the furniture for Christmas—an odd gift, she sees now, for a twelve-year-old girl. Her birthday gift that year is etched in memory. "They gave me a desk. The idea was, now that I was grown up enough to be studying and have homework, I needed a desk." The desk was "cute, really cute," she remembers. That is, for a museum or a furniture showroom. For a real, live girl it was hopeless. "It was a lady's writing desk, so it was teeny. You couldn't lay a paper on its surface." Even worse, "It was made of soft pine, so every mark I made went right into the wood." For Nicole, the desk symbolized the craziness of her life. "Here I was, trying to do my homework, and I was ruining this furniture, but furniture is more important than people, so how do I do my homework on this desk they gave me for homework, which ruins the desk that's more important than people? That's the kind of mixed up, convoluted confusion I was constantly in."

Although Nicole and her brothers weren't allowed to have pets, a black-and-white stray cat adopted them, Nicole especially. "The cat escaped one night and got into a fight," she says. "It got a sore on its side, and the sore got infected." For days, she begged her parents to take it to a vet. "'The cat will take care of itself. It will lick itself clean'—that's what they kept telling me," she says. Finally, the sore developed into such an enormous wound, seeping and dripping, and they could no longer ignore it. Nicole was waiting at the door when her mother arrived home from the vet's—without the cat. The infection had spread so much, her mother told her, the cat had to be put to sleep. After Nicole's father came home, the three of them drove to the vet's. She shakes her head at the memory. "Sometimes I don't believe their stupidity," she says. "They were successful, intelligent people, yet they were so stupid." The box her parents had brought to hold the cat's body was a flimsy little gift box, barely adequate for holding chocolates, let alone the weight of a dead cat. "I sat in the car while they went in to have the cat put to sleep," she remembers. "And they brought the cat out, dead, hanging out of this box, and presented it to me in the backseat, as if they were giving me a gift. They had this expectant look, like I was to be grateful. As if I should be thrilled to take this dead cat home and bury it."

Time has blurred the memory of what came next, but she knows she didn't cry. "You didn't do that, not in my family," she says. "If you cried, you were told they'd give you something to cry about." She was terrified that meant being given away—because someone in her family had. When she was eight, her parents adopted a five-year-old boy from Paraguay. "He didn't speak English and didn't conform to the image they wanted to project, so they gave him to the state after two years," she says. "I lived with that fear, if you don't fit in we'll give you away. It was very stressful."

Attempting to flee her parents' casual cruelty, she married after a year of college. It was to be the first of four marriages, the last of which was in its seventh year when her father's phone call came. She had moved to the opposite coast by then, trying to put as much distance as possible between herself and her parents. He needed an operation, her father explained, and didn't know who would stay with her mother, who was in the early stages of dementia. Yielding to the power he had always held over her, and as the only daughter, Nicole capitulated, and she and her husband, Jeff, flew there to help them. The surgery revealed terminal bladder cancer, and the hospital recommended a nursing home. But Nicole couldn't just abandon them. "Both of them were fully capable, physically," she says. "My dad was on his feet until two days before he died, and my mother had dementia, but there was nothing wrong with her physically." She decided to move in with them.

Asked why she would consider caring for two people who had treated her so miserably, she twists her hands and looks away. By this time, she says, she had discovered religion, and believed—misguidedly, it turned out—that she could model more loving behavior than they had shown her, and that they might respond in kind. She had another, more urgent wish. "It was my hope and dream that as they reached the moment of death, they might become real. I thought that by my serving them, they might have a moment of recognition of who I am." At the time, she didn't know, or didn't believe, that people die the way they live and that deathbed conversions are mostly the stuff of fiction. Her desire to see her dream come true overrode her common sense.

With only a few months to live, her father wanted to return to his boyhood home in Maine for a week to see it one more time. Nicole and her husband took him there. "He never said thank you, never ever, for anything we did," she says. Back home, sensing he was near death, Nicole made one last effort. "Daddy, I'd like you to say thank you for what we've done, for this trip to Maine." He began to wave her off, as he had always done. "Oh, you'll get it later . . ." he started to say dismissively. Then he appeared to collect himself, and nodded. "Thank you," he said briefly. It fell far short of the tearful reconciliation she had pictured, but it was something, Nicole felt. It was the only time he ever acknowledged her sacrifice.

Her mother never did, and maybe, Nicole thinks, after a certain point in her dementia it was unrealistic to think that she could. Still, against all reason, Nicole kept hoping for one moment of clarity. Her mother's dying took several years, and now, given the ill will that had existed between them for so long, Nicole wonders whether bringing her mother into her home was a good idea. Caring for her was much more difficult than she had anticipated. Nicole's upbringing had taught her to distrust her own perceptions (*Other people think we're so happy, so why don't I feel happy?*) and now, deciding what was best for her mother proved surprisingly difficult. The religious tenets that had motivated her to take care of her mother shrank against the reality of the woman who lay in the sickbed—the person Nicole blamed for everything bad in her life.

Four months before she died, her mother developed lung congestion, and rather than treat it Nicole decided to let nature take its course. But rather than worsening, the pneumonia became chronic. Although a physician examined her mother and concurred with Nicole's decision, as soon as he was out the door she found herself full of doubts. What is the right thing to do? she found herself wondering. Then the older woman seemed to forget how to swallow. A spoonful of food in her mouth sat there until it dribbled out—or her mother simply chewed and chewed and chewed. Feeding her took hours, so Nicole would put the tray down and leave. Her mother's mouth became dry and cracked, but she choked on the water Nicole tried to give her, so Nicole abandoned that effort. Again, hospice nurses affirmed that she was doing the right thing; she was the one with doubts. As December 1998 ebbed, Nicole found herself hoping that her mother would not live into the new year. When at last, toward the end of December, her mother died, Nicole wondered if she had killed her.

At first, Nicole felt only relief from the caregiving. She couldn't wait to get rid of the medical equipment and turn the sickroom into a bedroom again. But after a year, the feelings she thought she had overcome returned in a furious tide. "My parents' dying eliminated my fear," she says, "because it was too unsafe to bring anything up when they were alive. After that, I experienced all the hate and anger and grief of not having any possibility of a relationship." Now, added to the rage was the disappointment that neither one of her parents, despite her investment of time and care, had met her expectations of a final reconciliation, and now that possibility was gone forever. In addition to ruining her childhood, they had stolen a big chunk of her adulthood, too. And like icing on a bitter cake, she had the guilt of wondering whether she had caused her mother's death.

Nicole has found herself unable to forgive them, and the rage and disappointment she still carries around have interfered with her life more than she would have imagined. "It affects the decisionmaking I do every day," she says. "I'm applying for a more responsible position, but I find myself second-guessing every move I make. It's very hard to trust yourself when you've been taught to doubt reality all your life." She finds herself overreacting to small slights and struggles daily with self-esteem. "So the difficulties of daily living put a lot of pressure on me to come to terms with this," she says. Not surprisingly, her health has suffered, too, with skin ailments that don't clear and painful colitis. Nicole is working with a counselor, trying to excavate the self that's been buried for years—if it ever existed. She has come to understand that the one tool that would help her dig herself out of her past—trusting herself—is the one that was denied her by her upbringing.

In Julie Thompson's nightmarish childhood, the abuse was more overt. Her alcoholic father brutalized his five children physically and emotionally, and Julie's submissive, and probably terrorized, mother turned a blind eye. "We'd get cuffed or whacked," Julie says. "And he used to spank us with a belt. What happened was, my parents would become very angry at each other, and both would take their anger out on us kids." Her dad often told them they were stupid. "I was surprised, in my early twenties, when I took an IQ test and found out I was brighter than normal," Julie says. "I really believed I was stupid." When Julie was seven, her father raped her. To this day she doesn't know if he was merely drunk or in the middle of an alcoholic blackout—not that it matters. Her mother, returning from choir practice, cleaned the little girl up and roughly put her to bed. Afterward, she blamed Julie for the rape.

Her father's domineering personality ruled the household. He had inherited his family's small farm and worked on it, in addition to holding a full-time job at a local feed store. As soon as he returned home he'd start drinking. By dinnertime, Julie says, "he was usually crocked." She learned to gulp her food in order to escape her father's belittling. Forty years later she still finds herself bolting her food at times, a nagging reminder of her troubled childhood. "I mean, you'd say the sky is black and gray, and he'd say it is not, it's purple. He'd say anything to disagree with people," she says. Unlike Nicole's family, Julie and her siblings were able to confirm each other's sense of the craziness they lived with. It may have been their salvation, the one thing they could use to their advantage against him. For despite her father's efforts to turn one child against the other, she says, "We kids used to walk in the other room and laugh together, because it seemed unbelievable that he never saw the world or anything the same way anyone else did."

The hardest thing for Julie to forgive, however, has not been her father's blatant abuse but rather her mother's lack of support and protection. "My dad was especially shaming about my sister's and my sexuality," she says sadly. "I remember when I wanted to get my ears pierced. He told me only whores had pierced ears. I would have loved to have a mom who could have guided me as a young woman."

Yet astonishingly Julie has some good memories. While her father was mainly a source of fear, she credits him as the source of her spirituality. After he plowed the fields each spring in preparation for planting, he would take her on a treasure hunt. "My dad and I would walk the fields looking for arrowheads," she says. "There were lots of Indian tribes where we lived, and he would tell me about their customs and their connectedness with the earth. I still feel that connectedness, and it came from him."

After a disastrous first marriage made her take stock of her life, Julie enrolled in college to become a therapist herself. On her way to helping others, she worked on the rage she felt toward her parents. "I did lots of anger work," she says. In her study of family systems—the ways in which inherited patterns of behavior affect family relationships—she began to understand that both her parents came from abusive families of origin. Her father's family was especially sad, with a mother who married several times and had children from each marriage. "So, in my family, there was an ingrained feel to the abuse," she says. "Because there's a level of acceptance that passes from one generation to the next. I never knew it wasn't normal till I left home, got out and looked at other families, and visited friends in their homes."

Although she wouldn't know it until near the end of her mother's life, her mother also had been sexually abused by two of her six brothers, a fact divulged by her father during a family meeting. Gradually, the pieces of the puzzle began to fall into place for Julie.

Julie's growing independence as a young woman allowed her mother a new level of honesty with her daughter, freeing her to express feelings she'd kept inside for years. When Julie gathered the courage to leave her drug-addicted first husband, she says, "Mom told me she wished she'd had the courage I had, to leave a bad marriage. I felt she somehow lived vicariously through me, that I did some things she'd always wished she could do."

Julie's emotional evolution increased her compassion for her troubled parents. She eventually remarried someone healthier and gave birth to a daughter. Becoming a parent herself gave her new insight into the difficulties of parenthood. "I was determined to be the perfect parent, but I was not!" she laughs ruefully. "When my daughter ended up in treatment for some emotional issues, I thought to myself, 'Aha, I've done the best I can, and look at my kid.' That's the part that helped me begin the forgiveness process with my parents."

Years before her mother died of Alzheimer's and her father of emphysema, Julie wrote them letters in which she confronted them about the abuse. "They never responded, but I said those things to them, and I was always glad I did." The letter-writing, she realizes, was something she did for herself, not them.

But it has been Julie's recent breast cancer that has brought her to the final steps of reconciliation. With a life-threatening illness comes grief—grief at the loss of one's previous good health, grief at the prospective loss of loved ones, grief at the possibility of losing one's life. "I think the grief process flips us into a place of having to deal with unpleasant things," says Julie, who worked as a hospice counselor for several years. "Because grief doesn't just touch that particular loss; it calls forth every loss we've ever had. And it gives us an opportunity to finish up a lot of unfinished business, if we have the courage to go through it." For her, this meant reexperiencing her father's brutality and mother's betrayal—and laying it to rest at last. During a therapy session, she entered a state of deep relaxation in which she sensed her parents' presence. By then, they had been dead for several years. "I felt their agitation," she says. "They were acknowledging for the first time what they had done to me as a child, and asking my forgiveness." Because of all the work she had done—a lifetime's worth, really—she was able to free them and herself. "I told them I forgave them, and that I loved them both. It was very healing."

As Nicole's and Julie's stories show, there is often a great deal of unfinished business in the wake of a relief death, especially if it was sudden. Questions fly at us from everywhere, nag relentlessly, and refuse to go quietly: *Why were you driving to Buffalo the night of the accident? Will you please explain the separate bank account? Why did you leave the china shepherdess to her, when you promised it to me? Was your death really an accident?* And most haunting of all, *Why? Why were you so cruel, so abusive, so addicted, so uncaring? Why didn't you love me, when I loved you so much?*

No wonder telephone psychics and their ilk make millions of dollars each year. Particularly with sudden death, it's typical to hear, "I never got to tell him good-bye" or, "I wish I could apologize for how I treated her at the end." The finality of death allows no last-minute changes of heart.

It's tempting to think that long illnesses allow the luxury of tidying up all the loose ends, but this is sometimes wishful thinking. Not everyone chooses enlightened dying; some retreat into denial and silence. One man, diagnosed with terminal cancer, refused to discuss it, which precluded any long-term planning or hospice involvement. Even sadder, his silence made meaningful communication impossible. Words of love and gratitude went unspoken, forgiveness was not asked for or granted, no one said good-bye. Sometimes the nature of the illness prevents good-byes. One widow told us that her husband's dementia affected precisely the part of his brain that would have given him insight into his ALS. She says, "I felt really bad that we never, ever could talk about death and dying, or could say good-bye. I think I feel sad for all of us [she has two sons] about that. There was never that time when he could share what he appreciated about us and vice versa."

When the dying person is willing to acknowledge that time is limited, the rewards can be many. Hospice workers help families express Elisabeth Kübler-Ross's "four last things": thank you, I love you, I'm sorry, good-bye. Being able to tell someone how much they've meant to you, and hearing it from them, brings lasting peace and makes healing easier. Chris and Don and their children, Megan and Tim, were fortunate enough to be able to do this before Don died.

One of the popular myths surrounding death is that eventually, in order to move on, people obliterate the memory of the dead loved one; as one of Jennifer's clients asked on his first visit, "You're going to make me forget about my wife, aren't you?" Nothing could be further from the truth. We never forget; most of us wouldn't want to. Thane Brandt and his wife, whose infant son succumbed to a heart defect after birth, conceived a child shortly after Matthew died. Thane says that some people assumed the new baby would wipe the slate clean of Matthew's memory, a completely unwarranted assumption, as far as Thane was concerned. "One of the ladies I work with, I know she meant well," he says. "But she said, 'I'll bet you'll be glad when this next one is born, so you can move on.'" Poignantly, he says, "She doesn't understand that this baby will be a reminder. I know it will be one of the best days of my life, and one of the worst."

The task of grieving well is not about forgetting but about remembering in life-giving ways. As one grief counselor put it, "When I help people with letting go, I'm not talking about putting that person away. It's more like tucking that person into my heart and finding a place of value for them. I know they are still in my life, but not presently in my life."

Survivors of bad relationships must do this, too. But how is this possible when the person was such a negative influence and the memories are so full of pain? Relieved grievers are so overwhelmed by conflict, anger, and regret that they want to do nothing but heave a huge sigh of relief, slam the door, and padlock it. But it's essential for future relationships that they come to terms with the wretched relationship. The past is always with us in obvious and subtle ways; people with whom we have long-term relationships become, for better and worse, part of us. Gloria Reed found herself saddled with debt that her abusive husband, Nick, had incurred as a way of punishing her. Even something as innocuous as renting a movie—only to be told of Nick's delinquent fees—turned out to be a reminder of his vindictiveness. But that was minor compared to her son's express desire to emulate his stepfather when he grows up.

Unfinished business can take many forms. Particularly if the relationship has been lengthy, survivors may define themselves according to the way the deceased saw them. They still see themselves in the role of victim, and satisfactory grieving involves nothing less than creating a new sense of self. Similarly, someone who has been a longtime caregiver will find herself without a job and, consequently, without an identity. This may be part of Edna Matthews's problem. Her great relief at not being the subservient wife has unexpectedly become a stultifying lack of direction.

Surprisingly, indifference to a death can point to unfinished business, too, because it may mean feelings are being repressed. Even if the marriage was cold, or the relationship unloving, we need to grieve what we didn't have and what will never be possible now. "The grief is, many times, much greater for what we wish we'd had," one therapist wisely observed. Lenore Lansing, who felt very little emotion for her dead husband, found herself grieving heavily for the loss of the happy marriage that, as a young woman, she dreamed would be hers someday.

"The best way out is always through," wrote Robert Frost, and nowhere is that more true than after the death of a difficult person. Negative relationships generate negative energy, which must be transformed and redirected in positive ways, or else we become permanently stuck in the past. Some grief theorists, in fact, believe that we can't initiate satisfying new relationships until we resolve old ones—in other words, we can't say hello until we've said good-bye. The proof to Julie Thompson that she had at last laid her parents' ghosts to rest was being able to experience them as benign presences during chemotherapy for her cancer. "When I was sick last year, and I was very sick, I felt both my mother's and father's presence, fairly close. I felt that they were there and trying to support me from the other side. And that was very comforting."

That doesn't mean she doesn't feel some anger still, especially toward her dad. According to Lewis Smedes, author of *Forgive and Forget*, "Anger and forgiving can live together in the same heart. You are not a failure at forgiving just because you are still angry that a painful wrong was done to you." "Remember," he writes, "you cannot erase the past, you can only heal the pain it has left behind."

"The anger still comes up, it sure does," Julie acknowledges. To deal with it, "sometimes I journal, sometimes I talk with him." She chuckles. "I can cuss him out anywhere." Humor helps. At family gatherings, she and her sibs tell "Roy stories" about his unrelenting nastiness. With their newfound family unity, and because he is safely underground, they can laugh at him.

Julie experienced *Schadenfreude,* the happy-sad feeling survivors experience after a tormentor is dead. *Schadenfreude* can set our feet on the road to forgiveness, because we see that we finally have the upper hand; the person who has hurt us can no longer do so. According to Jeanne Safer, author of *Forgiving and Not Forgiving,* "An element of sadistic triumph is a necessary component of forgiving the unrepentant and the dead." Instead of living well being the best revenge, simply living, in these circumstances, will do the trick.

In fact, Safer believes that forgiving the dead is easier than forgiving the living. "After death, you can forgive without confronting the person, because you're not putting anyone at fault; you're only dealing with yourself." However, the physical absence of an opponent has its drawbacks: There is no longer any chance of apology or explanation. Your dead husband is not going to put his arms around you and tell you he's sorry; your dead mother is not going to invite you to climb into her lap. In ways that both simplify and complicate the process, the burden of forgiveness is on the one who is alive.

Anger is frequently part of the grief process and finds an endless number of targets. When the relationship has been loving, people blame the doctors who didn't diagnose the illness soon enough, the coworkers and friends who quit visiting, the insurance company who denied the operation, the clergy who ignored them. Because it's such an uncomfortable emotion to live with—exhausting, in fact—sufferers look for ways to rid themselves of it. Some try denial, which can lead to much worse consequences. Women, especially, who have been taught that nice girls don't get mad, may have trouble admitting the depth of their anger. Survivors of bad relationships may be rightfully angry at the abuser but instead turn the rage on themselves for staying in the bad marriage or tolerating the abuse, and thus the rage becomes depression. The new life they envisioned is empty of pleasure and purpose.

Some try to escape by using addictions. A counselor we interviewed said that many people she's worked have chosen a "spiritual bypass." "They go to their spirituality or a church and become overly involved," she says. "It's a way of not dealing with what has happened. They say, if I'm a good enough Christian, I don't have to feel bad about things I have done or that have been done to me." She notes that people can also do bypasses with drugs or alcohol.

But you can't run away from yourself. Death brings us our work, and how we deal with it determines our future happiness. Monica McGoldrick sees it as a matter of choice. "The question is, do you want to spend the rest of your life feeling bitter, or is there something else you want to do?"

she says. McGoldrick believes firmly that "acknowledging the truth of our history matters, because when we live in relation to our histories, our present and our future, we can make the best decisions." For Julie, making peace with her parents has led her to forgiveness; for Nicole Richardson, at least initially, it has taken the form of understanding, which she differentiates from forgiveness. Some experts, Safer among them, believe you can achieve emotional equilibrium short of forgiveness; it depends on the individual. Nicole says, "I have come to the point where I understand what made them what they were, and I understand their effect on me was not my fault," she says. Instead of forgiving them, she has put her efforts into forgiving herself, which some therapists feel is harder than forgiving others. "All my life, I've held such responsibility for my failure to make any of this work," she says. "I've begun to forgive myself because I understand it was beyond my power to do anything. It was absolutely beyond my reach." Nicole knows she still has a long way to go, whether the journey will end in forgiveness or not. "Because when, all your life, your reality has said 'you are wrong,' it's really a challenge to trust your own perception. It makes me think of the first time you get glasses; the world looks so different that, for the first couple of hours, it's hard to walk because you're not sure where the ground is. It's really easy for me to forget what I've learned and slip back into the old ways of being, that 'I'm wrong, and my way of looking at this can't be trusted.'" Nicole needs to be patient with herself. After all, she is only a few years into her journey, whereas Julie is twenty years into hers. Making peace with the past is a lifetime task, as Jennifer found.

Jennifer's story:

Paul died in February. By June I had moved to a larger city, and in August I started a graduate program in psychiatric nursing. I knew that my survival hinged on starting over in a new place, and I couldn't put enough distance between myself and the little town where my life had spun out of control so unexpectedly.

I guess I thought everything would be rosy once I had found an apartment for Elizabeth and me and started school. But peace proved more elusive than that. There were sleepless nights when I paced the floor, wondering why my marriage had failed and what that said about me. I took the phone off the hook for days because I didn't want to hear from anyone who offered sympathy, throwing me back into doubt and conflict. When people asked, I simply said I was a single parent. If I told them I was newly widowed, they gazed at Elizabeth and me with such sadness, I felt like a perfect hypocrite.

One evening, while browsing in the university library's card catalog, I found myself pouring out the story of my marriage to a fellow grad student who had a similar past and who was also reluctant to tell anyone about it. Nancy and I have remained the closest of friends for seventeen years, forever bonded by a similar disenfranchised grief experience. Unburdening myself to her, I see now, was my first step in coming to terms with the past.

Daily living, as well as dealing with troubled people in my practice, has helped me better understand the family and social influences that make us the people we are. As the cherished baby of seven older sisters, my upbringing was sometimes chaotic, but I always felt very loved and wanted by my mother and sisters. Because Paul had been an only child, I assumed he had been equally doted on by his parents and that he would lavish the same degree of affection on me that I would on him. Paul was my first serious relationship, and because I was a very young twenty-year-old, I had no inkling that everyone's upbringing hadn't been as unconditionally loving as mine. Looking back, I recognized that I had deliberately ignored some of the warning signs of his emotional instability.

It baffled and infuriated me that I missed him desperately at times. Songs on the radio made me ache inside, as well as the times when something made me remember his funny stories—he was a gifted storyteller and mimic. Sometimes I got impatient with myself for these contrary feelings. Accepting that they existed within me, right alongside my anger and relief, became part of my healing.

Even so, my journey wasn't over. Soon after graduate school started, I developed pleurisy and pericarditis, an inflammation of the lining of my heart and lungs. The intense pain in my chest radiated, terrifyingly, down my left arm, leaving me convinced that I was having a heart attack. I was irrationally certain that if I went to the emergency room I would die, too, just as Paul had—so I didn't go.

Thankfully, when I at last gathered the courage to see a doctor, a round of antibiotics cleared up the infection, but Nancy encouraged me to get some counseling, which she claimed was helping her. It was probably the best advice I've ever gotten. In those sessions, I was able to rant and rave and cry, cry, cry. Most helpful of all was the freedom to express the jumble of emotions I felt.

But although the sessions helped, I wasn't through with Paul, and it began to dawn on me that I never would be. However, I have been able to come to terms with my memories of him, and my dreams have been a kind of barometer of my healing. At first they were full of rage. Sometimes I slapped him and angrily confronted him with the all the pain he'd put me through. Being a very nonviolent person, I was horrified by these images. Through the years, though, the dreams have mellowed, and in a recent one he asked my forgiveness, and together we watched Elizabeth ride her mare. In thinking about this dream, I recognized that, without Paul, I would never have had my lovely daughter, and I smiled to think that this was his subtle way of reminding me of that.

Forgiveness has become a cultural imperative in recent years, with proponents claiming that those who can't, or won't, forgive will never find peace. But for some, finding meaning may be sufficient. "Meaning makes a great many things endurable—perhaps everything," wrote Carl Jung. This means honestly reassessing the past, to discover what gifts we gained from it, because there were some, no matter how unhappy it was. For Julie, the very spirituality that has helped her forgive was, ironically, a gift from her abusive father. Her own life experience has been invaluable in helping her treat her clients. "I help them recognize that they can feel more loved by the person who has died, and that may be a possible outcome," she says. "They can come to recognize that the person really did love them in their own way. To understand why someone is the way they are leads to compassion." The broadening awareness and maturity that living brings allow us to see patterns and incidents in ways that were obscured before.

Having landed safely also provides a springboard to forgiveness. Julie Thompson is successful in her career as a therapist and happily married, and after three false starts Nicole Richardson is at last in a satisfactory marriage. Proving the dead wrong by finding success in life makes reconciliation easier.

Beth Durkee still battles the stomach-churning emotions her mother-in-law's illness and death left her with. After Beth went away to gemology school, leaving her young sons in their father's care for most of a year, Ann froze her out of her life, but Beth never knew why. After Ann died, it was too late to find out. But Beth learned a hard lesson about unfinished business. "I have another situation like this ahead of me with my father. I cannot let him leave this world without getting some things straightened out because of what I learned from Ann. When someone dies, you've lost your chance to clear up anything. So if there is a relationship anywhere in your life, a close, intimate relationship, you can't just let it go and expect to find some kind of resolution. Things left unresolved are poison." And though her experience with Ann was anything but positive, what Beth learned will remind her to make different choices. Maybe, if she has a good outcome with her father, she'll be able to thank her hateful mother-in-law.

8
Honoring the Self

"*Sail on silvergirl,*
Sail on by.
Your time has come to shine.
All your dreams are on their way."
—Simon and Garfunkel

Jennifer's story:

In Virginia, Paul and I lived in a large colonial house splendidly set off by old azaleas and pecan trees. A charming feature of the house was the old wooden venetian blinds in each window—thirteen sets throughout the house. These were a constant source of angst for Paul. He wanted them all shut at night, and it was my job to open them each morning to let the daylight and breezes in. Before Elizabeth was born, Paul allowed me to work, and I was the patient-care coordinator in the cardiac unit at a hospital thirty minutes away. I left for work at 6:15 A.M. each day, and in my haste to get ready I didn't always pay proper attention to the angle of each blind. Instead of greeting me with a hug or smile in the evening, Paul often met me with a tirade. "Those look ridiculous from the road!" he'd scold, brushing past me to adjust the blinds. Only when he had them all calibrated to the proper angle did he relax enough to tell me about his day.

A few days after he died, I was sitting on the sofa, stewing in angry memories of his controlling ways, when my gaze fell on the hated blinds. Fetching a pair of scissors from the kitchen, I went from room to room, cutting each of them to bits. It felt wonderful.

Paul's taste ran to heavy, formal furniture and matching everything. My style is more shabby chic, and one time we had a huge argument over a tarnished silver celery tray. Somehow, I could never keep the proper "doctor's wife" image uppermost enough for Paul.

About a month after he died, I opened the door to some ladies from the Methodist Church who were asking for donations for a tag sale. They were open-mouthed when I offered them our thirty pewter Jefferson cups (traditionally used for drinking mint juleps), silver candlesticks and candy trays, two cherry end tables, and a matched set of dessert plates. I don't know who was happier about the transaction—the ladies, trying to conceal their delight at their good luck, or me, free at last of some of the awful reminders of my marriage.

The word "ritual" comes from "rite," a solemn, often religious ceremony, such as a wedding or baptism, or, following a death, a funeral or memorial service. In their adherence to certain prescribed steps, performed in a certain order, public rituals celebrate significant life changes, both pleasant and unpleasant.

As we've seen, funerals only do a so-so job of helping people grieve. Sometimes, the presider didn't know the dead, and the service has a generic feel; an awkward formality prevails that stifles any but the most stilted exchanges; decisions regarding flowers, music, location, or type of burial may not be what the survivors wanted; and in some rites, such as the Catholic funeral mass, personalization is discouraged, with emphasis placed on the universality of death and the hope of resurrection. But the primary drawback of funerals is that they happen only once, giving the impression that mourning ends, or ought to end, at that time, when in fact it is only beginning.

Yet funerals serve a valuable function in our increasingly death-phobic culture. They provide an opportunity for others to express grief; they bring the whole community together in both a symbolic and functional role to support those who have experienced a death; they provide a ceremony to delineate "before" and "after"; they help the bereaved assume the duties of their new roles; they provide a context for sharing memories of the deceased; they link the mundane with the eternal.

Private rituals are as meaningful as public ones. Almost every person we spoke to, whether the relationship had been happy or unhappy, had performed at least one private ritual as a way of "honoring the self." Mostly, these took the form of purging the environment of certain objects, as in Jennifer's case. Over time, certain items had become totemic of what was good or bad about the relationship.

Often, if the relationship had been troubled, private rituals were secret as well. Some felt that it was better to give away the dead person's possessions to relatives or charity, because a garage sale felt too public and might cause unflattering gossip. Some simply threw things in the trash—which had the advantage of being both private and satisfyingly vengeful.

Destroying the bad symbols while preserving the good ones provided a powerful way to begin to set things right again after a death. Just as public rituals invest certain objects with universally recognized symbolic value— flowers mean romance, beauty, and the promise of regeneration; wedding rings, eternity; white clothing, purity, innocence, and virginity; candles, warmth, light, eternity, and mystery—some objects acquire private meaning every bit as potent for the individual.

Chris's story:

I hated Don's wheelchair. For almost fifteen years of his life it was part of his body—although a despised part. While in many ways it made his life possible, it shouldn't have been anything a healthy young man needed. Maybe it was this ambivalence, which characterized so much of my life with MS, that made me loathe it so much.

It always seemed to me brutally unfair when it would malfunction, because it confronted me, yet again, with my helplessness against this illness. *Isn't it bad enough that Don's body isn't working? Do the replacement parts have to fail, too?* I would think. The temperamental beast had come close to ruining a couple of much-needed vacations. When Don's brother got married in Spokane, Don and I and the kids made the trip in our big brown-and-tan van, specially equipped with a wheelchair lift. We were enjoying visiting with Don's family when the chair decided to quit working, necessitating an impromptu trip miles across an unfamiliar city to get it repaired. Once, while the four of us and my sister Carol, who had come along to help, were visiting Canada, the batteries failed. Luckily, a local bike rental shop was able to find a battery that worked till we got home. Intellectually, I knew that mechanical equipment could fail; emotionally, having it do so in the midst of what should have been a carefree time for all of us reduced me to tears of rage and frustration.

Even before Don died, I'd had inquiries about the van, and it sold within a few days of his death. I ran an ad for the wheelchair in the paper, and a man called asking to see it. I was asking what I thought was a reasonable price for a top-of-the-line electric wheelchair, which had cost several thousand dollars brand-new, but when he said he would have to modify it to fit his sister, and asked if I would take a hundred dollars off the price, I readily agreed. All I wanted was to get it out of my house and out of my life.

Of course, if purging memories were as simple as purging objects, resolving a death would be a snap, and there would be no need for therapists and grief counselors. But for many people, purging was an urgent first step. In particular, reminders of an illness, such as sick-room equipment, mobility aids, and prescriptions, were quickly disposed of. Getting rid of such objects provided a way of clearing a psychological space that could now be filled with happier memories.

Many widows and widowers set about changing the physical space in their homes. Because we express our personalities in our choices of furniture and decor, our homes reflect our souls, so ridding an area of noisome reminders makes perfect sense. Even when the relationship had been happy, survivors felt a need to make a space their own again. When Don went to a nursing home, Chris replaced the bedroom carpeting. The carpet seemed to hold the dreary history of Don's illness: stains from the urine that had splashed from the urinal he kept by the bedside, as well as the bleach Chris used to disinfect it; a patch where the wheelchair battery charger had burned a hole in the carpet; black spots where battery acid had dripped; a path from the bed to the bathroom, worn by the heavy wheelchair tires.

Although most rituals arise after a death, they are equally valuable as a way of marking the ambiguous losses not seen as big enough to grieve by the community. Putting someone in a nursing home is one such loss, and one of Chris's ways of dealing with it was by doing some modest redecorating. Another way the family marked Don's move to the nursing home was with a ritual devised with the help of the hospice chaplain, which involved lighting four small, rose-scented candles in his room one evening. Chris and each of the children took theirs home; Don's remained in his room at the nursing home. The identical candles served to remind them that they were all connected by enduring emotional and family bonds; dividing the candles symbolized the ways their lives had diverged. Each could burn his or her candle as a reminder of each other, as well as of these contradictory truths.

The marriage bed is an obvious symbol of the marriage; small wonder that it is one of the first things to go. Chris sold the queen-size waterbed she and Don had shared and bought a daybed—in a twin size, just for her. Another widow replaced her bed frame and box springs and bought pretty linens and down pillows that expressed her preferences. Yet another widow simply reclaimed the bed psychologically. "The day he went to the nursing home, I just took off my clothes and got into bed," she says. "I realized I didn't have to keep one ear open for him, or one eye open on him, or have the TV going all the time, or set the alarm for his next set of pills. I realized it all at once, that I was not a prisoner to that routine anymore."

Going to bed alone in the empty house was especially luxurious for her because the house had seemed like a big sickroom for such a long time. "People would try to be nice, and they'd offer to come over and stay with Bill for an hour, and let me go out and 'do something I liked.'" she says. "But being sent out to the ladies' dress shop for an hour wasn't what I wanted! I wanted Bill out of the house!"

The walls of a home are seen as mysteriously absorbing the dead spouse's energy in ways that either comfort or disturb. Evelyn Washburn, whose husband abused her when he drank, didn't stop at their bedroom when she redecorated. "I redid my house," she says. "My mom came over, and we went through the house, getting rid of things. I got new bedroom furniture, I painted every room in the house. It made me feel a lot better, like it was my home, not my husband's. I reclaimed it."

Celia Schroeder, whose marriage to her husband, Ed, was long and happy, dismantled his small office downstairs and made it into a cozy sitting room. "I feel him down there where his office was," she says. "It's a comforting feeling." Dick Appling kept his office as it was, but it's also a poignant reminder of Marijane. "We turned one bedroom into an office, and Marijane'd be outside, doing something in the yard, or just walking around, and she'd open the door from the patio into the office, and she'd sit and watch me work at something," he remembers. "I'd pull a sheet out of the typewriter and show it to her, and she loved to read it, and would want to talk about it." Those memories fill him with sadness now. "I was typing away yesterday, and the wind pushed the door open, the same way." His eyes mist. "So that set off my day. . . . "

Gloria Reed's joy at being able to redecorate was especially exuberant because Nick had kept her under his thumb in that area, too. "I went hog-wild," she says. "Nick wouldn't let me express any of my taste in our home, or put up pictures of my family." The house is now full of green plants, photographs, and items that reflect her preferences. She was particularly glad to get rid of the sofa Nick had chosen and the kitchen canisters he insisted she use. She had a yard sale to sell those things, as well as Nick's clothes—which she didn't want in the house anymore. "They seemed contaminated with his bad energy," she says.

Nor are women, typically the "nesters" in a marriage, the only ones who undertake redecorating. Ken Nichols, whose mentally ill wife committed suicide, says, "She had lots of wonderful, expensive antiques, and I went through the house, tagging them. I asked my kids to go through the house and take what they wanted, and told them we would have an auction with what was left, and divide the earnings four ways. We tore the house apart." Getting rid of Eileen's possessions brought a welcome financial bonus. "At the auction, some of the stuff went to Sotheby's," Ken says.

Lenore Lansing says forthrightly, "I did a lot of purging." Her husband, Ed, was an avid hunter, and his hobby caused a lot of resentment. "It interfered many times with our social life. If he was going hunting the next morning, we couldn't go anywhere the evening before." Six months after his death, Lenore had "one of the biggest garage sales our town had ever seen." She got rid of his guns, his trophy heads, and his clothes. "He had beautiful clothes, and I thought someone should be wearing them. I gave them all to the Salvation Army." Not surprisingly, her actions raised some eyebrows in her small town. "Lots of people asked me, 'Don't you think you got rid of his things too soon?' and, 'Don't you think this?' and, 'Don't you think that?'" she says. "I just learned to say, 'No, it feels all right so far.' I developed that as my pat answer."

Of course, Lenore also performed the ultimate purge—she moved to another town, as did Jennifer and

several other widows. Leaving behind all possible reminders of the dead was a dramatic way of wiping the
slate clean and starting fresh, although, as she found, leaving the past behind is never as easy as simply relocating.

Not surprisingly, clothing is a potent symbol for
grievers. Evelyn Washburn got rid of all Mike's clothes.
"Mainly, they went in the garbage," she says. "It felt good
to get rid of all those things." Nicole Richardson, who
cared for her despised father during his bladder cancer,
didn't waste a minute, either. "The day after he died, I
was waiting for my brothers to arrive for the funeral. I
went into his room and cleared out his underwear
drawer." Her father had died of bladder cancer, and, she
says, "the smells were ghastly." He had remained ob-
streperous and emotionally shut down to the very end, re-
fusing to acknowledge the sacrifices she had made for
him, which compounded Nicole's need to cleanse the
house of reminders of him. She admits the choice of underwear is curious, and she wondered at herself. "Somehow, I took it all out on his underwear," she says. "I think
in part because it isn't the kind of stuff you give to someone else or sell. That was one thing that couldn't be put to
further use." His expensive clothing should be donated to
Goodwill, she realized, but the underwear could be gotten rid of immediately—and it was.

Hanging onto keepsakes that symbolize the good
times is equally important. Ken Nichols treasures a
Christmas ornament Eileen gave him. "I almost want to
be buried with that," he says. "It's a Christmas ball that,
when you pull the string, it plays 'Silent Night.' It's a re-
membrance of the good years."

Heather Harris and Kathy Brandt keep mementos of their babies' brief lives close by. Kathy keeps a picture of Matthew, who died of a heart defect, by her bed, and a ritual has evolved from it. One night after Matthew's death, while she was pregnant with her third son, she felt terribly frightened and vulnerable, "thinking I just could not bear to lose another child." She went into her room and kissed her picture of Matthew, then went in and kissed her son Zachary good night. "That's when I got a sense of peace," she says. Remembering that Matthew was now free of suffering, even though his life was short, reminded Kathy that Matthew was now in a safe place—and by extension, they all were. "I don't have to worry about him," she says.

Heather Harris arranged a little table with Joshua's things on it. Joshua died of a chromosomal defect four hours after birth. On the table, says Heather, are "casts of his hands and feet, a little outfit he wore, and a little hat, a stuffed animal he had gotten, his footprints and a lock of hair, and a rose we had gotten." Sometimes, she says, "I pick up his hand cast and hold it to feel how small it was . . . and having those things is really helpful."

Jewelry, especially wedding rings, is a reminder of promises kept or broken. Chris wears her engagement ring on her right hand, a constant sign of her love for her husband, and his for her. Many widows transfer their wedding rings to the other hand after a husband's death or have them made into other types of jewelry, which is what Jennifer did. After Paul's death, she couldn't wait to take her rings off—and did so almost immediately. As she rode home from the emergency room, she had a physical sensation of her own power returning. She took off her wedding rings and threw them into her purse. Eventually, she bought another diamond and had it and her engagement diamond set in a pair of earrings.

Kathy Brandt says, "On Mother's Day, Thane gave me a necklace with Zach's baby ring and Matthew's baby ring on it. I wear it every day, and every time I touch it, I feel two rings. This is a physical reminder to me that I have two baby boys. It helps to wear the necklace." Since their third son was born, she's added another ring to it.

Joan Nye never takes off a silver link bracelet made by a Native American artist. When her son, John, was in a wilderness program in Oregon, Joan swore that she would wear it until he got out of the program. When he did, she gave it back to him to wear, making him promise he wouldn't take it off until he finished high school; it became a symbol of their commitment to each other. Before he attempted suicide by taking a bottle of Tylenol and lying down in a field to die, John removed the bracelet, perhaps realizing that now he would never fulfill his promise. One of the teachers at his school found it and gave it to Joan. Today, the bracelet, always on her wrist, reminds Joan that she and John are linked together eternally in their love for each other. "Even during the bad years, we had a two-way connection," she says.

The ways in which people express connections with the dead are limited only by their imaginations. The beauty of ritual is that it can be molded to express the unique relationship that existed between the living and the dead. Stephanie Kellogg's mother, who died after a series of strokes, used to tell her that a surefire way to banish the blues was to paint your toenails bright red. After her mother died, Stephanie painted her mom's toenails with "Red Siren." But she didn't stop there. "At her memorial service, everyone—men, women, children, even the dog—wore red nail polish in her honor," she says. "One of my friends had had foot surgery, so we painted her bandage with red toenails." Even now, when she's having a bad day, she gets out the Red Siren polish she used on her mom's toes as a way to reexperience her mom's optimism and humor.

A woman Jennifer counseled, who had lost her twenty-two-year-old son to leukemia, was at a loss for a suitable way to memorialize him. After months of rejecting many ideas as not quite right, she hit upon one that seemed perfect. Her son had loved bow-hunting and had accumulated a number of expensive bows. Selling them, she used the money to buy 100 orange hunting caps embroidered with his name over the front. Then she distributed the caps, free of charge, to places issuing hunting licenses. She was delighted with her ritual. "Ben was happiest in the woods, hunting," she told Jennifer. Now, each year, she thinks of her son setting out, in spirit, with each hunter who ventures into the woods.

Rituals that take place outdoors are particularly numinous because of their connection to the eternity and grandeur of nature. Before he died, Don asked Chris to scatter his ashes in a beautiful valley in the Swan Mountain Range in western Montana, which the family used to drive through on their trips to visit his parents. Chris and her children held their own ceremony, during which they scattered his ashes at the base of a tall aspen tree. Chris still makes a point of laying a rose there whenever she passes the spot.

Rituals can be as elaborate or as simple as individual tastes dictate. Activities such as saying a prayer, leaving flowers, releasing balloons, and tending plants are some of the ways of remembering the dead. Both the setting in which ritual takes place, as well as the actions performed during it, remind us that as humans we participate in a universe reassuringly larger than our tiny selves.

Joan and Jerry Nye have improvised a ritual they perform on the anniversary of John's death. Joan says, "We have John's grotto, where John's two pets, Rascal, the darling little collie/cocker/beagle/dachshund he got when he was six, and Attila, the yellow cockatiel he got for his eleventh birthday, are buried. We have a cement bench, and some special plants, and I scattered some of John's ashes there, the part that didn't fit in the urn that is buried in Kalispell, with my grandparents." She writes a message to John, "We love you and miss you always," on a helium balloon, and she and Jerry watch it float out of sight. "I kind of talk to John," she says. "In my mind's eye, he can see me, and I think he knows how much I love him, and how much I loved him when he was alive," Joan says. Balloons are a favorite item in rituals because they convey images of freedom and release. They were used by several of those we interviewed who had lost children and babies to physical or mental illness.

While traditional funerals and memorial services are "rituals of connection," survivors of bad relationships will not draw much comfort from them because they don't reflect their truth about the relationship. Instead, disenfranchised grievers are often put to the torturous ordeal of sitting through effusive tributes to the person. "Just remember the good times," such grievers are misguidedly advised. Would that they could! Neither would it be safe to assume that those who are finally out of a bad relationship want to forget it completely, although some do. In fact, in their isolation they may be more in need of ritual than anyone. These grievers need "rituals of disconnection," which simultaneously honor their need to remember as well as disengage from their dead.

Sarah Langton, whose chronically depressed husband, Tom, committed suicide after years of threatening to do so, discovered an activity that honors both of them. She makes occasional visits to a park bench erected to Tom by the local Kiwanis Club, and her impromptu prayer goes like this: "I hope you're in a better place, because I sure am!" The bench provides a place of reflection for Sarah, as well as a place she can express her gratitude. Sarah's bench visits exemplify two of the best things about ritual: its flexibility, and its ability to express contradictory truths at the same time.

Often, rituals evolve spontaneously and then, if they prove satisfying, are repeated as needed. However, if a ritual hasn't sprung up that is meaningful to you, you might create one. In her 1998 book *Language of the Heart: Rituals, Stories, and Information About Death*, Carolyn Pogue tells the story of Barry and Anne, two children whose birth father had abused them. Eight months after their dad died in prison of a heroin overdose, their adoptive parents, enlisting the aid of a minister, helped them create a ritual for saying good-bye to him.

First, the minister asked Barry and Anne to make lists of both the good and bad things they lost when he died. Barry wanted his list to be "invisible," so that only he would know what was on it. He also wanted to read the story of David and Goliath out loud at the cemetery, because to him, it meant that "God doesn't always choose the big, tough guys to do his work. Sometimes little kids are important."

At the cemetery, the minister talked with the children about their lists and said a short prayer. Barry read the story of David and Goliath, then they burned Anne's list, along with some sweet grass, which the children, of Native American descent, recognized as a symbol of "cleansing, healing, and letting go." The family went for ice cream afterward.

Pogue stresses that the most valuable part of the ritual for the children was the process of thinking about their lives in relation to their father. Like other rituals, it provided some closure and resolution to what had been a painful relationship.

Effective rituals, like this one, employ as many of the five senses as possible. Fire, which appeals to all the senses, can be particularly expressive. It can be used to destroy something that sums up the relationship while simultaneously pointing the way to the future. One widow burned the journals she kept during her marriage. "I know I was grieving my marriage for a long time as I looked back on my old journals," she says. "By burning them, I got rid of the past."

A hospice therapist says that she sometimes facilitates rituals around letters and burning. "I'll have clients bring in a letter or a picture, and we talk about it, and then burn it." The letter provides a way to take stock of the good and bad things about the relationship, as well as a farewell. Burning it is a symbolic way of letting go.

Just as creating new rituals can help us come to terms with the past, endowing old rituals with new meaning is also important. To paraphrase one therapist, it can be a way of "tucking someone into our heart" and acknowledging the gifts that came from the relationship. Evan Imber-Black, author of *The Secret Life of Families*, writes, "When families cannot affirm their loss, their rituals become carefully staged events, lest the spontaneity and unconstrained human interaction inherent in authentic rituals lead family members to the unspeakable and the unknowable."

The ability to include the dead in family rituals is a significant sign of healing. Seventeen Christmases after Paul's death, Jennifer did something unusual: She hung Paul's china reindeer, Rudolph, with the chipped front leg, beside a china angel from her own childhood. At last, it felt right to include this reminder of her past in her present.

When Chris's daughter, Megan, got married several years ago, Chris was touched that Meg, for her November wedding, had woven her dad into the festivities. Don's Irish roots had been an important part of his identity and of family celebrations, and Meg had arranged for a bagpiper to play as the wedding party processed in and out of the hall; her wedding colors were Kelly green and white; as her bridesmaid gifts, she gave Irish *claddagh* rings; and, most evocative of all, a small lighted Christmas tree at the reception was a reminder of how much Don had loved the holiday. Like Tim's graduation three years after Don's death, it was a bittersweet day, but the reminders of Don reassured the family that he lived on in their happiest moments.

9

Moving On

"We must be the change we wish to see."
—Gandhi

The heady sense of relief following a death can fool us into thinking that the rest will be easy. Nicole Richardson vividly describes her reaction after the death of her mother, her last surviving parent: "At first we were waiting for the coroner to come, and I went into her room to look at her, and spent a moment feeling as though I should feel something, and not feeling much at this point. I got rid of the home health aide as soon as I could, then called the funeral home. It was probably forty-five minutes to an hour before they came. I just waited calmly for the process to be done." Then came the rush she had waited for so long. "When that gurney crossed the threshold of the front door, I could feel, literally, the child inside me jump for joy. It was a physical feeling, and I could see this child with her arms in the air, just jumping and dancing for joy. It blew me away. I just staggered back and said 'whoa. . . . '" Later, when the feeling faded, Nicole wished that she had, in fact, danced. "I wish I had allowed myself to mirror that feeling with all of myself. Instead, I kind of clamped down, just noted it, and continued to process it for the next few weeks—the depth of freedom that child felt. Maybe one of these days, I will do that actual dance of joy with all of me."

Unfortunately, the ecstasy didn't last. Within a few months, Nicole's memories of life with her narcissistic parents came to the forefront, and she still deals with an acidic backwash of anger.

Jennifer, too, felt an initial rush of power:

> Although I would have preferred to be alone, I allowed a member of the rescue squad to drive me home from the emergency room. As we drove in silence, I was aware that, in a split second, everything had changed. I experienced a physical sensation of the strong, confident, healthy parts of myself returning. "The Yankee is back!" I told myself, as I squared my shoulders and sat up straighter. I was vibrantly aware that a dark chapter in my life was closing. As if to mark its finality, I took off my wedding rings then and there.

After a relief death, the future, which at first seems to unroll before us like a smoothly paved road, turns out to be full of potholes. What we envision as we sit at the bedside of a loved one can feel quite different after the bed is empty. We don't immediately comprehend the ways we have been changed. As one widow complained, "I thought I'd be out tripping the light fantastic." Instead, her life had faded to gray, and she didn't know why. "I'm afraid I'm wasting my life," she admits. "There's something missing. I have these 'shoulds.' I 'should' be doing this or that or the other. There's this feeling that I 'should' go out and do something creative or helpful or something, and that hangs over me."

"What are you going to do now?" well-meaning friends and relatives ask, and we are uncomfortably aware of having no answers. Instead of feeling free of the duties that used to structure our days, we may feel rootless and unnecessary. Adele Bachmann, whose mother, Catherine, was seriously handicapped for sixteen years when a blood clot during surgery caused a serious stroke, reflected after her mom's death, "It's almost shocking, the totality of it—the physical work, the legal and medical papers to be filled out, buying the food, taking care of the doctor's appointments. I don't think people have any appreciation for what's involved. But when you stop doing all that stuff, you don't know what to do with yourself." A few weeks after her mother's death, she was reminded of how totally immersed she had been in her mother's care. "The phone rang one night at midnight, and I jumped up, thinking that something had happened to Mom," she says. "It's when all the activities around death have stopped that you feel relieved. After that, you have all this time, but you don't know how to function."

Yet during a lengthy illness we have a chance to make life changes while the person is still alive—and we may be much readier to move on than those dealing with a sudden death. Because Don had been in a nursing home for five years, in many ways Chris was living as a single person when he died and was way ahead of most widows in the adjustment process. Those who have done a great deal of anticipatory grieving sometimes must educate well-meaning professionals who haven't quite caught up. Chris had to explain her situation to hospice counselors offering follow-up care and turned down invitations to join support groups. When someone has done most of their grieving before the death, there isn't as much need for such ministrations. Ken Nichols had a similar experience after his wife, Eileen, committed suicide. He remembers, "Shortly after she died, I heard about this widow/widower support group up the street, so I went up there to see what was going on. It was a group of people who'd had similar experiences. I was the only one with a suicide. Most everyone else in the group was in real acute, sad grieving, so it was a little bit different."

In the elderly, the loss of caregiving duties can turn into a genuine identity crisis. Dick Appling, eighty years old when his wife died, says, "My distress was so great, over such a period of time, that now I kind of feel like I'm dancing on air, feeling like all my responsibilities ended with Marijane." On the flip side, his choices are by no means clear. Marijane had Alzheimer's, and Dick's life for the past eleven years was devoted to her care. "I did have some serious doubts whether I wanted to go on after Marijane died," he says. "I'm honestly quite sure I'd never do suicide. That's a coward's way out. But I think I could go anytime I want. I'd just have to give up. It's not going to be that quick, but you know, in a relatively short time . . . So I'm experimenting, trying to find out if I'm worth a place in the universe yet." He isn't satisfied just passing time. "I play bridge a couple times a week, go out and eat lunch with my friends, but that's not a reason for living. There's got to be something that you do, something that you want to do, that if the world doesn't appreciate it now, they may one day." Facing such a challenge at an advanced age takes real courage.

If the relationship has been bad, anger can keep us from looking ahead. "People ask, if I've been married to this person I hated for forty years, and I'm having such a good time now, what kept me from leaving sooner? Why did I waste so much of my life?" says Ken Doka. Even if the relationship was not one of choice, a son may ask how he could have allowed himself to be baited into that same stupid argument with his dad every time; a sister, why she kept trying for closeness with a sibling when the door remained locked and bolted. Beth Durkee blames herself for not detaching from the dance of anger she found herself in with her mother-in-law. Those who are having trouble finding direction may have hidden anger, which can masquerade as depression. One widow, whose husband's chronic illness increased his abusiveness, admits, "I am really angry, because I thought that the day he died, I would put all of it behind me. It hasn't worked out that way. I have this hangover of a depression and have been diagnosed with post-traumatic stress disorder from living with him. I have flashbacks and nightmares."

Evelyn Washburn, whose husband, Mike, abused her and their two boys, found she'd lost trust in men. "My boys tell me I will never be able to have another man because they don't want another man like their dad, so angry and mean." Her boys aren't the only ones who have doubts about her ability to choose a better partner. "It would take me a long time to trust another man," she says. Certain areas of one's life take longer to heal than others. On a positive note, Evelyn has returned to school to study computers and is coming to see herself as someone with something to offer the world.

Nicole Richardson has found that she has had to devote a lot of time to exorcising her parents' legacy. "The past year has been heavy and deep, not playful and light like I thought it would be," she says. "The thorn removed from the side reveals the infection that has gone so deeply. A lot of time has gone toward digging deep in the wound and getting out the infection." At the same time, however, she is aware of a sense of freedom. "I felt like I was really finally free to pursue all my areas of interest, and really pour myself into expressing myself, which had been limited simply by their existence on earth. I think those limits held, even though I was in Montana and they were back east."

Death can unleash creativity, sometimes in part because of a desire to prove the dead wrong. Joy Stephens, whose parents were constantly disappointed in her refusal to be a staid citizen like them, decided to be as different a parent from them as she could possibly be. "Every year for Christmas, I still get a game for my kids, who are thirty-one and thirty-five! We love to play games," she says. As for herself, at age fifty-six, she still has a keen sense of adventure. "I love to downhill ski, I took up archery, last year I got an elk. I intend to be active as long as I'm able."

Paul told Jennifer she was stupid and would never get a graduate degree; determined to prove him wrong, she obtained both a master's and a doctorate—all while parenting a young child. He spurned her sexually and made her feel unlovable; today she is happily remarried to a man she met three years after his death and with whom she has a son. For both good and bad, Paul has had a profound influence on her life:

Jennifer's story:

In my marriage, I nearly lost track of who I was, and the experience has influenced me in a number of ways. I've decided never to make my children, my strong-willed daughter in particular, feel ashamed of having a passion for people and life, as I had been made to do. I'm perhaps a little more tolerant of my children's rebelliousness because I'm so aware of the effects of trying to conform to someone else's image.

Having to live a lie in my marriage has made me value truth highly. This expresses itself in a number of ways. I believe I am a better nurse, counselor, educator, and human being because I value honesty. I feel it's always the better choice, because we keep people stuck in the role of victim if we tiptoe around the truth. Writing this book has been one way for me to tell my truth, and, I hope, help others to tell theirs.

Staying connected with others, which those in bad relationships sometimes forfeit for the sake of peace, as I did, is critical for optimum mental health. One reason I felt so oppressed in my first marriage was that Paul isolated me from the normal "mirrors"—the friends and family we all use to assess our behavior, appearance, opinions, and values. Paul became my only reflection, and because I hardly ever met his rigid expectations, I was always doubting myself. The lesson I've drawn from this is to never again allow myself to become isolated from friends and colleagues. Today, I constantly seek out old and new friends for support, laughter, and validation.

Last, I have an "attitude of gratitude" toward my second husband, Brad. Not a day goes by that I'm not grateful for his kindness, his sense of balance, his healthy ego, and his belief in my abilities and encouragement of my goals. I'll never take him for granted.

Human beings constantly search for meaning in the bad things that happen to us, and we may find our previous belief systems don't hold up anymore. Chris's belief, which she discussed in her book *Surviving Your Spouse's Chronic Illness*, is that the experience of being a well spouse should become a spiritual journey; at the least, those who find themselves in the grueling, and sometimes thankless, role of unpaid caregiver need to find meaning in what they're doing. Being a caregiver is hard enough; feeling your efforts are futile makes an already difficult job more difficult still.

Finding meaning is not necessarily the same as finding rewards. Americans love the myth that caregiving is spiritually uplifting, that family members are somehow ennobled by the experience. Most caregivers would disagree. We do what we must, in part because we would want someone to care for us if the shoe were on the other foot. Expecting caregivers to care perfectly, beautifully, patiently, quietly, indefinitely—in other words, beatifically—is profoundly unrealistic. And expecting those who must watch helplessly as a loved one dies to feel enriched by the experience is just plain absurd.

The paradox that Marla Mabry spoke of following Tiffany's death is a real one. "How can I say that I'm relieved that the burden of caring for my child is gone," she asked, "when it isn't supposed to be a burden?" As Marla knows, the perception of caregivers as saints makes the relief afterward a dirty little secret.

Although our culture tends to see death and bereavement in strictly negative terms, there is a richness to the grief process that is seldom acknowledged. We learn things about ourselves we would not have discovered any other way. And we can draw valuable lessons from the dying.

Chris's story:

During the storm and stress of the caregiving years, I felt too depleted to do much more than put one foot in front of the other. The "rewards of caregiving," if they can be called that, I have discovered largely in retrospect.

I am deeply grateful for the way Don accepted his move to a nursing home. Although he could have become resentful and critical, and blamed me for the decision, he showed a generosity of character that kept the four of us close till the end. Once, when fourteen-year-old Megan said to him tearfully, "Daddy, this is a terrible place," he shook his head. "No, it's like a big hotel," he smiled. He hated it there and would have given anything to be home, but he was careful not to let the children know the extent of his distress.

These could have been dangerous years for the children; Meg was fourteen and Tim was eleven when Don went to the nursing home—old enough to begin getting into real trouble. It didn't happen. During these traumatic years, both children remained studious, law-abiding, and mostly dependable. Meg went off to college several hundred miles away, a year before Don died, in large part because he encouraged her to pursue her own life.

As hindsight made these miracles—and they were indeed small miracles—evident, I recognized that Don's acts of kindness drew us all closer during his illness and have kept us close since his death. Nine years later, the three of us talk about him freely and remember him with great love. Both my children have decorated their living spaces with photographs and mementos of him. Don's gracious acceptance of his fate, his faith in God, and his unflagging hopefulness were a few of the gifts he left us.

Marla Mabry says that her daughter Tiffany's compromised existence taught her that life doesn't have to be perfect to be fulfilling. "I look at her life and think, it's kind of existential, but you can't really live until you accept the inevitability of death. The point is to live a good life, to live until you die. And I kind of think that Tiffany was reaching a point where it wasn't going to be a good life anymore."

Thane Brandt had a similar epiphany because of the time he shared with his gravely ill son, Matthew, who lived only two and a half hours. Thane remembers that in the delivery room, "The doctor said he'd be pink, but he was blue and not making any noise. The doctor asked me, 'Do you want me to do anything?' and that was really hard for me, but I said no." He and Kathy had agreed beforehand not to use any extraordinary means to keep the baby alive. Then, surprisingly, Matthew "pinked up" and began to breathe. "There was no wailing cry like with other newborns, but he was a pretty normal baby," says Thane. Like his wife, Thane says that the two hours Matthew was with them were "wonderful. For twenty weeks [after they found out about the heart defect] it felt like someone was standing on my chest," he says. "The sense of relief after he came was tremendous, to see him and love him." Thane believes that allowing Matthew to be born, then let nature take its course, was the best decision they could have made. "We were offered termination when the heart defect was discovered," he remembers, "but the way we looked at it was, in utero, Matthew was perfectly fine and healthy. His problems wouldn't start until after he was born." It was a decision they look back on with gratitude, because, Thane says, "We created a vessel for his soul, is how I look at it. I made it possible to see my son again someday."

Kathy conceived again shortly after Matthew's death—and had very mixed feelings. "Two weeks after we found out [about the pregnancy], we were going to Great Falls to see his grave, and I was having an awful day," she remembers. "It felt like déjà vu, because it was the same time of year I was pregnant with Matthew. I was terrified of it happening again." Matthew's grave had a clover patch, and the couple began to search for a four-leaf clover. "I said, 'Thane, have you ever found a four-leaf clover?' and he said, 'No, do they even exist?' I said, 'I know they do, because people always find them—but I never have.'" They were astonished to find a five-leaf clover in front of the headstone. Kathy thought she saw a significance. "Counting this baby, there are five in our family. When we looked closer, there were two big leaves and three little ones, and the little ones varied from big to little to tiny, and the middle one, Matthew's, had a hole in it. You could actually see it." Kathy knew it was a gift from Matthew, "saying this is how it's meant to be, there's supposed to be another one in this family, and everything's going to be okay with this baby. It's been his strength that's kept me going." Just as she predicted, their new son is fine and healthy.

Thane adds, "I can't help but think that we owe this third baby to Matthew, because we might not have had this baby otherwise. We were only going to have two. And now I get to have three kids instead of just two."

For some, gratitude turns into a quest to help others in similar bleak circumstances. Heather Harris is starting a support group for other grieving parents. In a letter to us, she enclosed a verse from Corinthians that reads, in part, "Praise be to the God of all comfort, who comforts us in our troubles, so that we can comfort those in any trouble. . . . "

Sometimes we grow not by learning lessons from the dead but by dealing with the aftermath of a death. Laura Archibald began going to Al-Anon in the mid-1980s, never expecting that its principles would someday help her resolve a difficult death. In those days, her nineteen-year-old daughter, Terry, had begun dating a methamphetamine dealer, and soon, to Laura's despair, Terry was doing meth herself. When Laura and her husband, Dan, committed Terry to a drug-treatment program, they were advised to attend Al-Anon as a way of dealing with the crisis. Laura remembers their first Al-Anon meeting. "We went around the circle, and said what we were there for. I was surprised that Dan said anything, because he's usually pretty reserved. He said, 'We're here to help our daughter, Terry.'" She laughs ruefully. "Boy, did they set him straight!" After the meeting, she and Dan had the same reaction. "We said, 'What strange people! All they talk about is themselves!'" Both Laura and Dan wondered what the point was in going if it wasn't going to help Terry, the focus of all their agony. Instead, as they discovered, the twelve-step program of Alcoholics Anonymous (AA) and its offshoot, Al-Anon, is designed to help the participants.

"They teach that there's a higher power that has some kind of loose control," Laura says. "I wasn't religious, but I had no difficulty thinking of a higher power." The corollary to that—and the idea that was most helpful to her—is that everyone in the universe is on his or her own path.

She admits that it sounds simple but is actually very diffi-cult to put into practice. "Instead of looking at the other person and yourself, alone in this struggle," says Laura, "you can say that the other person is on her path, and I'm on mine, but it's not my job to control them, or dictate how they behave." That's because, ultimately, "their higher power will take care of them."

Blessedly, everything worked out for the Archibalds. Terry got clean at rehab and, to her parents' shock, ended up getting several of her friends off drugs, too. She dropped the meth dealer. And Laura and Dan learned a helpful new philosophy. "I never worked the twelve steps in any consis-tent way," Laura says, "and even though the program, strictly speaking, is designed for the families of alcoholics and drug addicts, it has continued to help me. You come to a life experience, and the teaching suddenly makes sense. You go, 'Aha, that's what they meant by that.'"

The biggest test of this came two years ago when Laura's schizophrenic older sister, Linda, died in a distant state. Because Linda had been mentally ill, her abusive-ness over the years had been easier for Laura to accept, but the relationship had been very rocky. "I was raised to be protective of her, although at times I wanted to kill her," Laura says. "She was physically abusive. She'd lose it, get angry, and hit me."

Laura's worries increased after her parents, who had lived in the same town as Linda, died and her sister be-came even more isolated. "Here she was, thousands of miles away, and there was nothing I could do," says Laura. "She was an adult, so I couldn't have her commit-ted, but she had no one else, no husband, no family. I felt so helpless, and so angry at the system. As long as you can stand up and walk around, there is no help for mentally ill people in this country." Incredibly, Linda was still able to work as a bookkeeper, and she seldom missed a day of work. "Schizophrenics have this incredible energy," Laura explains. "She worked so hard." She continues, "She probably could have made much more money if she'd invested it, but her paranoia kept her from doing that." Linda's death at fifty-two came as a horrible shock to Laura, as much for its unexpectedness as for the circumstances. Linda died on the floor of her apartment, unable or unwilling to summon help. By the time her landlady discovered her, Linda had been dead for several days. "To think of a sister of mine dying in a filthy apartment was unbelievable," Laura chokes. "Of course, there were elements of relief, although the overwhelming reality was extreme sadness."

Laura's distress was compounded when she learned she was the sole beneficiary of her sister's estate. Linda's single-mindedness had helped her amass the tidy sum of $47,000. But Laura, far from being delighted, was anguished. "She had worked so hard for that money," she says, "and I felt so sad that she would never get to enjoy it."

She found solace in the principles of Al-Anon. Her sister was in the care of a higher power, just as Laura herself was, she realized. "The more you think about others in terms of a higher power, the more peace you have," she says. "It helped me forgive myself for not being able to help her more. Al-Anon teaches that we're here to lend a helping hand, but not to meddle. And I certainly tried to lend a helping hand, even if I wasn't very successful."

Ken Nichols took up drinking as a way of coping with his wife Eileen's mental illness. "For years, she would hide out in her drug of choice, and I would hide out in mine," he says. "Now that she's gone, I don't have to do that anymore." He quit drinking a year and a half before Eileen's suicide, and though he feels that Alcoholics Anonymous ultimately saved his life, initially its principles were not at all easy to embrace. "I got sober in January 1994, and they asked me to turn my life and will over to a higher power," he says. "Well, I wasn't about to do that, because, after all, I was a doctor and I knew best." He smiles. "Well, AA said, that's not going to work." His resolve to attend the meetings and live according to AA principles was tested at every turn by Eileen, who felt threatened and constantly tried to thwart him. He remembers his turning point. "I was out walking about 6 A.M., and it was very, very windy, and the candy wrappers and the leaves were blowing along the side of the canal, and there was no water in it. It was very bleak. I looked up, and in one of the trees, there were a couple of crows, cawing like hell. They were trying to fly and they couldn't take off, it was blowing so hard. I looked a little bit further down the path, and there was a hawk sitting in a tree. He was gripping the tree, I saw his talons, then he let go and spread his wings, and he didn't have to make any effort at all. He was lifted with that wind, and taken wherever the wind wanted him to go. I realized I didn't have to try, I couldn't, because I couldn't make any headway. Letting go of my desires, of believing I knew best, and just spreading my wings, was my spiritual awakening."

His sobriety survived Eileen's suicide, his own open-heart surgery, and a stroke two years ago that paralyzed the left side of his body—and from which he has recovered, all without drinking. He insists he is not religious. "I live right around the corner from a radio station, and there are four radio towers there. I walk every morning about 4 A.M., and I look up there, and the red lights are blinking on and off, and I think about that as being my higher power. He is always there, and all I have to do is tune him in. Even when it's foggy and cloudy, like it was this morning, I know he's there."

Because it is so hard-won, spirituality that is forged during desperate times is uniquely meaningful. It hasn't been handed down, or learned in a classroom; it's been paid for with our own tears and trials. It feels "earned."

Adele Bachmann says, "I have to tell you that I had two moms, the one before the surgery, and the one after. They were both wonderful." She believes that her mother died twice. "The first time, after the surgery, was terrible, there was no relief that she wasn't suffering. She just lived in hell, it was so difficult. The second time, her actual death, was a relief."

For Adele, Catherine's death wrought permanent physical as well as spiritual alterations in her life. "You reclaim your life, but it sure isn't the life you started with," she says. Adele does things more slowly, for one thing. "Someone said to me once, 'Your mother moves like the *Queen Mary*. She seems to be moving slow, but she gets there before anyone else.'" She says, "I walk slower now, because I walked with her." In the empty fields around her home, she finds an apt metaphor for the year following her mother's death. "When you plant winter wheat, you look around, everything is bleak. You plant it, and nothing happens, except that you know it's there and still alive, and when you least expect it, the following spring— there it is!" She believes she will see her mother again, "probably after I'm reborn," she says. "I think life is a circle instead of a line. Things go around."

Is there a harsher reality than witnessing the death of someone we want desperately to save? It's so hard to imagine any good coming from something so ugly.

Yet as with other painful experiences, there is opportunity here.

C hris's story:

After a certain point in my husband's illness, I had to face the fact that my love could not save him. He would succumb to this disease. Still, I could not believe that that would be the end of this man I'd loved so much, who had been so much more than his body. Leaving aside the idea of whether I would see him again in the next life, I believed that some part of him, and of all of us, survives the body's disintegration. Eventually, I came to trust the teaching of the resurrection.

During the years of Don's illness, the New Testament story of Lazarus became my favorite, because so many elements seemed to fit Don and me. Lazarus had been a good friend to Jesus. I could easily imagine that, if we had lived in Jesus's time, he too would have enjoyed Don's company, because many people did. In the gospel story, Mary, Lazarus's sister, sends for Jesus when her brother becomes ill, but Jesus delays. When he finally shows up, it's too late. Mary is distraught. "Lord, if you'd been here, my brother would not have died," she tells him. I knew exactly how she felt. Many times I'd asked myself, *Where is God in this mess we've wandered into? What can he be doing that is more important than curing my husband?* When he hears that Lazarus has died, Jesus weeps. But as everyone knows, the story has a triumphant ending, with Jesus calling the dead man from the tomb. When Lazarus appears, wrapped in a winding sheet, Jesus tells Mary and Martha, "Unbind him, and let him go free." Those words came back to me in the days after Don's death. I imagined Jesus saying the same words to Don, who was now free of the flesh that had kept him earthbound. On the brass plaque I ordered to place on the tree in the Swan Valley, I had the chapter and verse of the Lazarus story engraved: JOHN 11:1–44.

Jennifer's story:

Something else happened the night Paul died. As I gazed up into the clear, dark, winter sky, I saw a glorious shooting star cross the heavens. I was astonished and mesmerized; I had never seen such a thing before. In spite of my ambivalence about Paul's death, I felt very comforted by the rocketing star. He had been so troubled; I felt that it was a message from him, telling me that he was in a better place, that I should move on.

Although I had been raised Catholic, I had long doubted the existence of any one all-powerful deity. To me, religion was a fear-based style of interacting with the world, and I had stopped going to church as soon as I left home. However, after seeing the star, I began to think that there was something beyond myself I had been blind to. Now, living in Montana, I often see shooting stars cross the heavens. Every time, I'm reminded of Paul and the possibility that our spirits—and the spirits of human beings everywhere—remain connected even after death.

If nothing else, we have learned about our complexity as feeling, thinking, human beings. We know that fiercely opposing emotions can live within the same heart. Marla says slowly, "I think it is just . . . I don't know what it is. There are things you are supposed to feel, and people spend a lot of time trying to feel what they are supposed to feel instead of accepting what they do feel, you know."

Notes

⌒⌒⌒

Chapter 1: Speaking Ill of the Dead

p. 10. "Kathy Charmaz, professor of sociology at Sonoma State University . . ." Charmaz, Kathy. *The Social Reality of Death*. Reading, MA: Addison-Wesley, 1980, p. 203.

p. 11. "British grief researcher Colin Murray Parkes . . ." Parkes, Colin Murray, P. Laungani, and B. Young, eds. *Death and Bereavement Across Cultures*. New York: Routledge, 1997, p. 236.

p. 11. "Wittily, Judith Martin (Miss Manners) calls the funeral . . ." Martin, Judith. *Miss Manners' Guide to Excruciatingly Correct Behavior: The Ultimate Handbook on Modern Etiquette*. New York: Galahad Books, 1991, p. 689.

p. 11. "According to Kenneth Doka, senior consultant to the Hospice Foundation of America and professor of gerontology . . ." Personal interview with the authors, January 25, 2002.

p. 12. "Doka believes there are three types of disenfranchisement . . ." Doka, K. J., *Disenfranchised Grief: Recognizing Hidden Sorrow*. Lexington, MA: Lexington Books, 1989, p. 4.

p. 12. "In an article for *OMEGA: Journal of Death and Dying*, Charles Corr, professor emeritus of philosophy . . ." Corr, Charles. "Enhancing the Concept of Disenfranchised Grief," *OMEGA: Journal of Death and Dying*, vol. 38, no. 1 (1998–1999): 1–19.

p. 15. "Ironically, etiquette maven Judith Martin seems to have the most realistic picture . . ." Martin, Judith. *Miss Manners' Guide*, p. 694.

p. 18. "Cultural historian Philippe Aries has noted . . ." Aries, Philippe. *Western Attitudes Toward Death: From the Middle Ages to the Present*. Trans. P. M. Ranum. Baltimore: Johns Hopkins University Press, p. 87.

p. 19. "The authors of one book confessed . . ." Nolen-Hoeksema, Susan, and Judith Larson. *Coping with Loss*. Mahwah, NJ: Lawrence Erlbaum Associates, 1999, p. 144.

p. 19. "Noted grief researcher Therese Rando . . ." Rando, Therese A. *Treatment of Complicated Mourning*. Champaign, IL: Research Press, 1993.

p. 20. "At long last, that approach may be changing . . ." Carr, Deborah, et al. "Marital Quality and Psychological Adjustment to Widowhood Among Older Adults: A Longitudinal Analysis." *Journal of Gerontology: Social Sciences 2000*, vol. 55B, no. 4 (2000): S197–S207.

Chapter 2: Altruistic Relief

p. 24. "She wrote about the dying patients she observed in her work . . ." Kübler-Ross, Elisabeth. *On Death and Dying*. New York: Macmillan, 1969.

p. 25. "Maybe the ultimate testimony to the popularity of her five-stage model . . . " *The Simpsons*, created by Matt Groening, Fox-TV.

p. 26. "For her doctoral dissertation in 1991 . . ." Elison, Jennifer C. K. "Reactions to Spousal Death Resulting from Cancer: A Descriptive Study of Anticipatory Grief and the Cognitive Appraisal of the Loss of a Spouse." Unpublished diss. in partial fulfillment of the requirements for the doctorate of education degree, College of William and Mary, Williamsburg, VA, 1991.

p. 27. "At last his wife, Aurora, goddess of the dawn . . ." Hamilton, Edith. *Mythology*. Boston: Little, Brown, 1942, p. 428.

Notes

p. 28. "However, the results of a multimillion-dollar study conducted by the Robert Wood Johnson Foundation . . ." Oddi, Lorys F., and Virginia R. Cassidy. "The Message of SUPPORT: Change Is Long Overdue," *Journal of Professional Nursing,* vol. 14, no. 3 (May–June 1998): 165–174.

p. 32. "Public opinion surveys show that most Americans are more afraid of pain than death . . ." Study by the Robert Wood Johnson Foundation, *AARP Bulletin,* vol. 43, no. 1 (January 2002).

p. 32. "Unfortunately, according to a recent report by AARP, most doctors . . ." Study by the Robert Wood Johnson Foundation, *AARP Bulletin,* vol. 43, no. 1 (January 2002).

Chapter 3: Dual Relief

p. 53. "Andrew Solomon, author of . . ." Solomon, Andrew. *The Noonday Demon: An Atlas of Depression.* New York: Scribner, 2001.

p. 59. "Therese Rando states that any illness lasting more than eighteen months . . ." Rando, Therese A. *Grieving: How to Go on Living When Someone You Love Dies.* New York: Bantam, 1988.

p. 59. "A large study undertaken by the Institute for Social Research . . ." Carr, Deborah, et al. "Psychological Adjustment to Sudden and Anticipated Spousal Loss Among Older Widowed Persons." *Journal of Gerontology: Social Sciences 2001,* vol. 56B, no. 4 (2001): S237–S248.

Chapter 4: Relationship Relief

Interestingly, Sigmund Freud didn't seem unduly troubled by his own nontraditional loss response. In 1930, his ninety-five-year-old mother, Amalia, died. Although Freud had been extremely distraught at the earlier death of his four-year-old grandson, writing "I don't think I have ever experienced such grief," he found his mother's death, by contrast, liberating. He was somewhat puzzled by this reaction, writing that he found it "curious." However, he had worried about dying before his mother, because she would have grieved deeply at the death of her firstborn and favorite child, her "Golden Sigi." He explains his own lack of grief as due to "[her] great age and the end of the pity we had felt at her helplessness." He wrote that he felt "no pain, no grief," only "a feeling of liberation, of release." Cited in Walsh, Froma, and Monica McGoldrick, eds. *Living Beyond Loss*. New York: W. W. Norton, 1991, pp. 115–116.

p. 81. "Modern theories of psychology owe a great debt to British psychologist John Bowlby . . ." Bowlby, John. *Attachment and Loss*. New York: Basic Books, 1969.

p. 82. "Psychologist Colin Murray Parkes found that certain bereaved people . . ." Parkes, Colin M. *Bereavement: Studies of Grief in Adult Life*. Madison, CT: International Universities Press, 1987, p. 142.

p. 82. "In an intriguing article . . ." Wortman, Camille, and Roxane Silver. "The Myths of Coping with Loss," *Journal of Clinical Consulting Psychology*, vol. 37, no. 3: 349–357.

p. 83. "As one popular book advised . . ." Tatelbaum, Judy. *The Courage to Grieve*. New York: Harper and Row, 1980.

p. 87. "In *The Corrections*, Jonathan Franzen's National Book Award–winning saga of a Midwestern family . . ." Franzen, Jonathan. *The Corrections*. New York: Farrar, Straus and Giroux, 2001.

p. 89. "Author Catherine Sanders, developer of the 'Grief Experience Inventory,' writes of a seventy-five-year-old widower . . ." Sanders, Catherine. *Grief: The Mourning After*. New York: Wiley, 1989, p. 217.

Chapter 5: Guilt

p. 93. "Chris recently received a letter praising her 1999 book . . ." McGonigle, Chris. *Surviving Your Spouse's Chronic Illness*. New York: Henry Holt, 1999.

p. 112. "Therese Rando writes, 'It is a cruel trick of human nature that, in the early phases of mourning . . .'" Rando, Therese A. *Treatment of Complicated Mourning*. Champaign, IL: Research Press, 1993, p. 481.

Notes

p. 114. "I think anyone who thinks they should seek counseling . . ." Kenneth Doka, personal interview with the authors, January 25, 2002.

Chapter 6: Social Support

p. 122. "Charles Corr writes, 'How many times . . . '" Corr, Charles. "Enhancing the Concept of Disenfranchised Grief." *OMEGA: Journal of Death and Dying*, vol. 38, no. 1 (1998–1999): 1–198.

p. 123. "Leave it to Doonesbury cartoonist Garry Trudeau to rush in . . ." *Doonesbury*, October 9–11 and October 15–18, 2001.

p. 127. "Kathy Charmaz, professor of sociology at Sonoma State University, believes that what we grieve after a death . . ." Charmaz, Kathy. *The Social Reality of Death*. Reading, MA: Addison-Wesley, 1980.

p. 134. "Sociologist Monica McGoldrick, associate professor at the Robert Wood Johnson Medical School . . ." Personal interview with the authors, May 17, 2002.

Chapter 7: Unfinished Business

p. 153. "According to Lewis Smedes, author of *Forgive and Forget* . . . " Smedes, Lewis. *Forgive and Forget*. San Francisco: Harper and Row, 1984.

p. 154. "According to Jeanne Safer, author of *Forgiving and Not Forgiving* . . . " Safer, Jeanne. *Forgiving and Not Forgiving: Why Sometimes It's Better Not to Forgive*. New York: HarperCollins, 1999.

p. 155. "Monica McGoldrick sees it as a matter of choice . . ." Personal interview with the authors, May 17, 2002.

Chapter 8: Honoring the Self

p. 175. "In her 1998 book . . ." Pogue, Carolyn. *Language of the Heart: Rituals, Stories, and Information About Death*. Kelowna, British Columbia: Northstone, 1998.

p. 177. "Evan Imber-Black, author of *The Secret Life of Families*, writes . . ." Imber-Black, Evan. "Rituals and the Healing Process."

NOTES

In *Living Beyond Loss.* Ed. Froma Walsh and Monica McGoldrick. New York: W. W. Norton, 1991, p. 213.

Chapter 9: Moving On

p. 183. "People ask, if I've been married to this person I hated for forty years . . ." Kenneth Doka, personal interview with the authors, January 25, 2002.

Index

68890